THE
THEOLOGY OF
MARCUS GARVEY

Roderick Michael McLean

UNIVERSITY
PRESS OF
AMERICA

Copyright © 1982 by **Roderick Michael McLean**

University Press of America, Inc.

P.O. Box 19101, Washington, D.C. 20036

Printed in the United States of America

ISBN (Perfect): 0-8191-2336-6
ISBN   (Cloth): 0-8191-2335-8

Library of Congress Catalog Card Number: 81-43759

Dedicated to the Garveyites----

   dead, alive and unborn--who
keep the flame of hope ablaze. God
is not finished creating us yet!

   May the spirit of Marcus Garvey
in us live on!

ACKNOWLEDGEMENTS

I would like to extend sincere thanks and
gratitude to my wife Dorothy and daughter Rebecca for
their patience and understanding during the many
hours, days, and weeks that I had to devote exclusively to the work of research and the writing of
this dissertation. I will always cherish their
thoughtfulness.

A special word of thanks to Father Richard Smith,
S.J., former chairman of the Department of Historical
Theology at St. Louis University, for his counsel and
confidence in me upon my entering the Doctoral
Program at St. Louis University. I am also indebted
to Sister Joan Range, my adviser, for her encourage-
ment and insistence on a high level of intellectual
and scholarly approach in my research. It is with
deep appreciation that I welcome her presence on my
Doctoral Committee, along with Dr. Lawrence O'Connell.
I was specially delighted that Dr. Douglas Meeks,
Professor of Social Ethics at Eden Theological
Seminary, accepted the request to serve as Director
of my study. I am indeed grateful for his guidance
and resourcefulness.

My gratitude also to the staff at the Schomburg
Center for Research in Black Culture, Harlem, New
York, for their patience and helpfulness in providing
me the necessary assistance in the gathering of my
research data. I want to express thanks also to my
step-son, Reverend Charles Stith, Unison United
Methodist Church, Boston, Massachusetts, for affording me access to his library collection of books on
Black History and Black Theology, and the healthy
dialog which helped me to clarify some portions of
the dissertation.

Finally, a word of gratitude to Major Clarence
Tolbert, a leader of the Garveyite Chapter in
Chicago for providing me with rare copies of the
Universal Negro Catechism, The Universal Book of
Ritual, The Universal Negro Improvement Association
Constitution, as well as affording me the opportunity
of interviewing him. Thanks also to Mrs. Arthella
Jennings of Gary, a widow of a former Garveyite, Mr.
Edward Jennings, Assistant to the International
Organizer of the UNIA, 1929, who provided me with
copies of personal correspondence, journals, news-

paper clippings and other helpful information. I had the pleasure of interviewing Mr. Alex Oliver, a Garveyite who also resides in Gary. I am indebted to these persons who were associated with the Garvey movement for providing me with such valuable resources and insight into the Garvey movement. I will treasure the Garvey papers as a part of my library collection.

Above all, to the secretary, Brenda J. Humphrey, for her dutifulness in typing this manuscript, I thank you for a job well done. To my friends, and well-wishers, too numerous to mention, who prodded and encouraged me, through their prayers and inspiration, to complete this project, I say thanks to all of you.

Roderick McLean

TABLE OF CONTENTS

A Foreword to
THE THEOLOGY OF MARCUS GARVEY
by
Roderick M. McLean

This book by Roderick McLean represents the first quality attempt at developing a full scale Theology of Marcus Garvey. It is an important contribution to the broad expressions of Bl.ck Theology and meeting the need for a full and more completed development of the thoughts of a person who has such great influence on the current world-wide Black Awareness Movement.

We do not think of Marcus Garvey as a devout churchman or a perceptive theologian as he is being presented for these pages. There is a tendency to think of him as a social or a political activist, without reference to his theological motifs.

Dr. McLean rightly contends that Garvey was the pre-eminent Black Theologian who sought to formulate a theology of history which he insisted was essential for the Black people's of Africa, America and the world to recognize their full humanity in blackness.

From a Black frame of reference, Dr. McLean contends that "Garvey's Theology" grew out of an exegesis of Black existence and from the divine perspective--God, as Creator of all humanity in equal status.

In one part of the book, Dr. McLean's study is most helpful because it set Garvey's thought in historic perspective and makes it relationally relevant to the current conditions of slavery in America and current African Zionism of the time.

In part two of the book, Dr. McLean gives an informal and informing discussion of Garvey's concepts of God, Christ, man, salvation and redemption.

In part three Dr. McLean gives a helpful discussion of Garvey's influence on current Black theology and to the current Black Liberation Struggle now in focus worldwide, with a special emphasis on the current Black condition.

ix

For persons who have not taken Garvey's thought serious heretofore, this will be a most rewarding introduction.

Dr. Major J. Jones
President-Dean
Gammon Theological Seminary
Atlanta, Georgia

INTRODUCTION

It is time that the theology of Marcus Garvey be lifted out of the rhetoric and propaganda of the Black movement in American History and become systematic and scientific. To this end I dedicate this dissertation. Garvey has been an active collaborator and pioneer in the struggle for the freedom and advancement of his race, and therefore had no qualms about defining God, Humanity, Christ, Redemption in the light of the historical experiences and needs of his own people. His distinctive contribution was to cast all of his religious reflection upon the experience of a people in the appropriate institutional form which he himself characterized as "one great Christian Confraternity" without regard to any particular denomination and which can be called a form of "Ethiopianism." In this sense Garvey was the pre-eminent Black Theologian who formulated a framework based on a philosophy of history which did not simply dwell on the achievement of Blacks in past history, but also the future redemption of Africa as a means of gaining full humanity.

His theology was based on an exegesis of Black existence both in its chronological and cultural essence, and from the divine perspective - God as Creator of all humanity in equal status. In place of an ecclesiology Garvey stressed the concept of the Kingdom of God as a cooperative venture between God and His people, in that wherever and whenever the power and potential of God meet the obedient action of a people a new set of circumstances are created in keeping with the true origin and destiny of that people. It was his relativism, coupled with his ineradicable belief in the transcendent and a vision of a monumental view of history that prefigured his theology. I will endeavor to show that Garvey was conscious of a historical continuity in the spiritual/cultural experience to an authentic sense of national identity, hence the call for a spiritual and cultural rejuvenation - "Up, You Mighty Race." It is within this chronological and cultural course of human history, and specifically the history of the Black race, that Garvey addressed the theological issues of self-identity - Who am I? Who is my God?

Garvey's theology is based on a firm doctrine of the goodness of creation and the accessibility of the commandments of divine goodness to the human situation. He saw human culture as a process within and part of

a wider cosmic process. It was not simply the wistful
projection of his own wishes and beliefs in what the
Black race can achieve, rather, Garvey affirmed the
Doctrine of God as Creator of all humanity, and saw
the Black race in their present state as having their
origin in God, and therefore potentially good or
"mighty". Garvey not only used the human race, an
anthropology, as a point of departure, but African
culture as a source of solidarity, of symbols, rituals,
philosophies and ideologies, and of common belonging-
ness. His interest in the Black race was not simply
past-oriented but directed towards the future; not
simply what Blacks were like, but how can Blacks make
the best of their present human resources, which are
largely traditional. In that sense he posited a
theology that was pragmatically satisfying and not
merely theoretically enlightening.

If one way of viewing contemporary theology is as
a critical reflection on praxis, then the theology
of Garvey can be viewed as a critical reflection on
the Black race's role in human/divine history, inasmuch as Garvey's theology did not lead to his
commitment and action but is rather a reflection on
it. Moreover, if the function of theology is to
assist the confessional community in arriving at a
viable self-understanding in its given situation and
to relate itself to that situation then the theology
of Garvey can add to an analysis of the signs of the
times for Black America, and the demands with which
they challenge the Christian community to be faithful
in the liberating/redemptive process.

It is not my contention to propose a corrective
to contemporary Black theology. Rather, I am propos-
ing a theology that begins from a different point of
departure. In contemporary Black theology too much
emphasis, with the exception of Albert Cleage's Black
Messiah and Black Christian Nationalism, is placed on
the victim. For example, the prevailing captions of
contemporary Black theology are "God of the Oppressed",
"Black Suffering", "Liberation From Oppression", "A
Theology of the Slaves", etc. In addition, the use of
the "oppressor-oppressed" model, which seeks a balance
of power, or the sharing of power, or redistribution
of power, seems to be the dominant theme for most of
these theological works. Perhaps, the theology of
Garvey based on themes such as "God as Creator", "God
as Sovereign Power", "Up, You Mighty Race", "African
Redemption", "A Theology of the Here", "The God of

Equality", "Conscience of Equality", "Glorification of The Black Race", etc., can serve as a creative and innovative force for regarding Blacks as subjects of their history rather than always as objects and victims. Garvey called Black people to see themselves as they were meant to be, and as such did not seek to elevate the Black race above others, based on a concrete historical experience - The Mighty African Empire, and rooted in the transcendent reality of a Mighty God, Creator of all humanity. Garvey not only articulated the theology, but as a practitioner he sought to overturn, challenge, and transform the religious perspectives and ecclesiastical institutions of his day.

It is the thesis of this study that Marcus Garvey, an early Black Mass Leader, posited a pragmatic and internally consistent theological framework by which to interpret the meaning of his people's origin, history and their destiny. The context for this approach is found in an exploration of the roots of Black Zionism in the United States of America in the latter nineteenth century, and the historical watershed in the Black experience known as the Harlem Renaissance in the early twentieth century. It was during the Harlem Renaissance period that the United Negro Improvement Association (1918-1927) was developed. This movement, headed by Marcus Garvey, provided the platform for the articulation and development of the Theology of Marcus Garvey.

This contribution of the theology of Marcus Garvey becomes more than an intellectual quest, rather the purpose of this dissertation is to add to the cumulative effect of Black scholarship, and to provide continuous spiritual nourishment of our cultural past.

Chapter I

THE CONTEXT FOR A STUDY OF GARVEYISM

A. The Rise of African Zionism in the Latter
    Nineteenth Century

The nineteenth century was probably the most
humiliating and degrading century in the history of
the Black race. The African slave trade which had
reached a new zenith in the eighteenth century
continued to flourish, despite the well-intentioned
efforts of the British to stop it and the legal
prohibitions imposed upon it by European and American
nations. A vast contraband trade supplied the huge
demands for slaves on the plantations of the Americas.
On the western coast of Africa this was not
rigorously brought under control until the 1860's.
In these same years in East Africa, the Arab trade
in ivory and slaves caused widespread and
unprecedented devastation. Not until the last decade
of the century was the slave trade successfully
combatted. Africa, in the meantime, had 'bled her
life's blood at every pore, ' and need resuscitation.

In the New World, the beginning of the century
saw the vast majority of Negroes in slavery. Although
the system had been abolished in the British West
Indies in 1834, and in the French and Danish West
Indies in 1848, it continued a vigorous life in the
United States, Cuba and Brazil. The roots of slavery
had been so firmly planted in the southern region of
the United States of America that it took the Civil
War (1861-1865) to bring about its abolition. In
Cuba and Brazil, the final emancipation, Blacks of
the New World were, for the most part, regarded and
treated as less than equals to whites, and were not
accorded the full status of free men and women.

The Black World of the nineteenth century was
worst for the Blacks in the United States. Whereas
in Latin American countries slaves possessed rights
both by law and custom, and manumission was widespread,
in the United States under white domination slaves had
no rights either in law or custom: they were mere
chattels. West Indian Blacks, including Marcus Garvey,
were fortunate in being the first in the New World to
gain their emancipation. In contrast, the condition
of Blacks in the United States was steadily declining

from the early part of the nineteenth century to the outbreak of the Civil War. Hollis Lynch, in his documentary of the lot of Black Americans in the nineteenth century focused attention on a major issue of the period:

> But perhaps the greatest wrong inflicted on the Negro Race in the 19th century was the successful building up of a myth that the Negro was inherently inferior to other races - a myth that had been originally elaborated in an attempt to justify Negro slavery, and later, European imperialism in Africa . . . but it was the vigorous humanitarian campaign for the abolition of slavery which spurred slave holders and their supporters to defend the institution by asserting that the Negro was an inferior being, and that slavery was actually for him an elevating process. By its repetition, the myth-makers and their descendants came actually to believe that the myth was true.[1]

This myth of the inherent inferiority of Blacks was further strengthened and perpetuated in the latter part of the nineteenth century with the rise of social Darwinism, with its theme of the survival of the fittest. This philosophy further reinforced the myth-makers and provided ready justification for European imperialism in Africa.

It was the humiliating condition of Blacks in the New World which spurred Edward Wilmot Blyden (1832-1912), the Pan-African Patriot, to becoming the greatest champion of the African Zionist Movement in the nineteenth century. However, it is important to realize that the vision of a regenerated Africa originated in the late eighteenth century with the influential British evangelical and humanitarian movement which directed its energies against slavery and the slave trade - and towards the 'civilization of Africa through Christianity and commerce.' The founding of Sierra Leone in 1787 was the first practical manifestation in Africa of this influence. Even

---

[1]Hollis Lynch, Edward Wilmot Blyden: Pan-Negro Patriot (London, 1967), p. 13.

before Blyden, other New World Black leaders had de-
vised or supported plans which they hoped would bring
dignity and respect to their race. Because the condition of the Blacks in the United States had been
the worst, it was from among them and West Indian
Blacks who had experienced American discrimination
that African Zionism, also referred to later as Pan-
African nationalism, emanated. In the first three
decades of the nineteenth century four outstanding
and dedicated leaders - Paul Cuffee, Lott Cary,
Daniel Coker, and Jamaican born, John B. Russwurm -
advocated and delineated the emigration of Free
American Blacks to Africa. These men held visions of
progressive nations rising on the African continent,
and, all but Cuffee, played prominent roles in the
early history of Liberia.

Significantly, it was in 1808 that Paul Cuffee,
the first American Black leader to champion 'repatriation', made his first inquiries about Sierra Leone.
Cuffee was greatly influenced by the prevailing ideas
for the 'regeneration of Africa'. Among his plans
were the promotion of selective American Black emigration to Sierra Leone, the suppression of the slave
trade, and the inauguration of a vast trade between
Black America and West Africa, designed to enhance
the wealth and prestige of the race. Cuffee was also
interested in an intensive program of Black education
as a necessary pre-requisite for the building of
sovereign new nations in Africa. In the light of
these goals, Cuffee made two trips to Sierra Leone in
1811 and 1815, and carried over thirty-eight Black
Americans largely at his own expense. Cuffee's trips
had important consequences. They demonstrated the
feasibility of colonizing free Black Americans in
Africa, and the idea was earnestly taken up in America
by a curious combination of the humanitarians and the
slave-holders. These two incongruous elements founded
the American Colonization Society in 1817, and their
efforts led to the establishment of Liberia.

However, it was Edward Wilmot Blyden who eloquently articulated the objectives of the philosophy
of African Zionism in the latter nineteenth century.
He sought to persuade Black Americans that it was part
of a 'grand Providential design' that they should return and help in the civilizing of Africa; they were
to do so before it was 'usurped' by Europeans. To
this transcendental argument, Blyden added a plea
based on racial pride. In the wake of the upcoming

Garvey movement in the early twentieth century, it is important to note the groundwork that was laid by his predecessors, and particularly Blyden who in an address in 1862 before a group of Black Americans, entitled "The Call of Providence to the Descendants of Africa in America" said in part:

> An African nationality is our great need . . . We shall never receive the respect of other races until we establish a powerful nationality. We should not content ourselves living among other races, simply by their permission or their endurance . . . We must build up Negro states; We must make and administer laws, erect and preserve churches . . . We must have governments; we must have legislation of our own; we must build ships and navigate them; we must play the trades, instruct the schools, control the press and thus aid in shaping mankind. Nationality is an ordinance of Nature. The heart of every true Negro yearns after a distinct and separate nationality . . . Liberia, with outstretched arms earnestly invites all to come. We call them forth out of all the nations; we bid them to take up their all and leave the country of their exile . . . We summon them from the States, from Canadas, from the West Indies, from everywhere, to come and take part with us in our great work . . .[2]

But the stirring pleas of Blyden and other Liberian commissioners were to no avail. For, appearances to the contrary, the outbreak of the Civil War was the signal for dropping schemes for emigration of Black Americans.

If Blyden's Pan-African ideas are one of the main historical progenitors of Pan-Africanism, it was perhaps in Marcus Garvey's Back to Africa Movement that

---

[2]Ibid., pp. 29-30.

the greatest heritage of his ideas is to be found.
When Blyden died, Garvey was a young man of 25 years,
and although so far no reference has been found to
Blyden by Garvey, it seems likely that the latter who
was a voracious reader of works on or by Blacks, was
well acquainted with the writings of Blyden. At any
rate there is a marked identity of views between the
two West Indians: both claimed to be 'pure Negroes',
and were intensely race-proud; both supported New
World Black repatriation to African and envisaged that
continent as the scene of future glory for the Black
race.

     In tracing the rise of African Zionism in the
nineteenth century in the light of the humiliating
lot of Blacks in the New World, one cannot fail to
note the crucial role of religion in the struggles
towards freedom, identity, and self-determination.
The people of the Black Diaspora, uprooted and thrown
into the New World cauldron and melting pot, have had
to grapple for centuries with the problem of how to
preserve their dignity and self-esteem in situations
where white men held them in slavery, and then, when
emancipation came, refused to accord them the full
status of free men and women. The more reflective
among them have also been obsessed with the question
of "Who are we?" and "Why have we suffered this fate?"
Black Americans had to come to grips with the dual
problem of uncertain identity and powerlessness. They
knew they were Africans and "of African descent", but
white men invested the name of Africa with attributes
that brought on feelings of shame. Compensatory beliefs backed up by convincing authority - great myths,
the source of every people's deepest strengths - were
needed to bolster their self-esteem. Consequently,
Black people under slavery turned to the Bible to
"prove" that a Black people, Ethiopians, were powerful and respected when white men in Europe were bar-
barians. Ethiopia came to symbolize all of Africa;
and throughout the nineteenth century, the "redemption
of Africa" became one important focus of meaningful
activity for leaders among New World Blacks.

     This focus on "the redemption of Africa" came
about as a counter-measure to the myth of Black
inferiority which was being perpetrated by the
slaveholders. White Christians in the South attempted
to strengthen their control over the minds of the
slaves by tightening up the supervision of their religious training, including attempts to prevent slaves

from holding worship unless white people were present.
Some Southern theologians were also circulating
manuals with material for masters and mistresses to
read to their slaves, containing admonitions such as:

> Almightly God hath been pleased to make
> you slaves here, and to give you nothing
> but labor and poverty in this world,
> which you were obliged to submit to,
> as it is His will that it should be
> so. Your bodies, you know, are not
> your own; They are at the disposal
> of those you belong to . . .

> When correction is given you, you
> either deserve it or you do not
> deserve it. But whether you deserve
> it or not, it is your duty, and Almighty
> God requires that you bear it patiently . .3

The Black preachers, whether literate or
illiterate, whether they believed in insurrections or
did not, whether they approved of emigration or
disapproved, felt impelled to counter-attack on a more
basic front. They were not only convinced that God
would eventually destroy the slave system in one way
or another, but also that the Bible did not support
the position that Black men were cursed or inferior.
Out of their offensive efforts a retrospective myth
of eventual divine deliverance took form, backed up
by Biblical "proof-texts". Black Folk Theologians
were able to find the texts to counter the derogatory
scriptural interpretations. As soon as they became
aware that Egypt and Ethiopia were in Africa, they
were able to preach and teach along these lines.

It was during this period of identity crisis
that there arose the development of a mode of thinking
called "Ethiopianism" and the concept of "Providential
Design". Both of these concepts were later expanded
by Marcus Garvey and formed the basis of his
theological system. This thought-style that was
called "Ethiopianism" emerged as a counter-myth to
that of Southern White Christians, and many Northern

3St. Clair Drake, The Redemption of Africa and
Black Religion (Chicago, 1970), p. 47.

ones. It functioned on a fantasy level giving
feelings of worth and self-esteem to the individual,
but also as a sanction for varied types of group
action. It generated concern for the "redemption of
Black people in the Motherland Africa as well as in
the New World, so that the ancient state of power and
prestige could be restored. Among the many sermons
of Black Preachers, reference was made to this hope
of "redemption of Africa:"

> God's own chosen people had to go into
> Africa once, long ago, when the famine
> came, and Joseph became a great man in
> a Black folk's kingdom . . .

> And as for the Ethiopians, they were
> the darkest of all, for did not the
> prophet Jeremiah ask 'Can the Ethiopian
> change his skin? Can the leopard
> change his spot? . . .'

> We were not always white men's slaves and
> our time will come again, for the Bible
> says, 'Princes shall come out of Egypt
> and Ethiopia shall soon stretch forth
> her hand unto God . . .[4]

This Biblical myth was a comforting morale builder and
steeled those Black people who believed it against
those who tried to 'rob them of their past.' Edward
Blyden further gave impetus to this concept of
"Ethiopianism," and even broadened the scope of its
significance when he wrote:

> Africa may yet prove to be the spiritual
> conservatory of the world. Just as in
> past times, Egypt proved the stronghold
> of Christianity after Jerusalem fell,
> and just as the noblest and greatest
> Fathers of the Christian Church came out
> of Egypt, so it may be, when the civilized
> nations, in consequence of their wonderful
> material development, shalr have had
> their spiritual preceptions darkened and

---

[4]Ibid., p. 49

their spiritual susceptibilities blunted
through the agency of a captivating and
absorbing materialism, it may be, that
they may have to resort to Africa to
recover some of the simple elements of
faith; for the promise of that land is that
she shall stretch forth her hands unto
God.[5]

It was Blyden's view that the exiled Black has a
home in Africa, and he is entitled to a whole
continent by his constitution and antecedents. Since
the book of human civilization is not closed, one
can contend that there is still hope for the exiled
Black American. The vision is still alive today,
though it may be blurred.

The concept of "Providential Design" which
undergirded the call to African Zionism was ardently
espoused by a Black American, Alexander Crummell, in
1853. In a sermon delivered in Monrovia, 40 years
after the establishment of the republic, he gave
eloquent expression to this doctrine, referring to:

. . . the forced and cruel migration of
our race from this continent and the
wondrous providence of God, by which
the sons of Africa by hundreds and by
thousands trained, civilized, and
enlightened, are coming hither again,
bringing large gifts, for Christ and
His Church, and their heathen kin.[6]

He envisioned Black history rising to a climax:

The day of preparation for our race is
well nigh ended, the day of duty and
responsibility on our part, to suffering,
benighted, Africa, is at hand. In much
sorrow, pain, and deepest anguish, God

---

[5]Edward W. Blyden, Christianity, Islam and The
Negro Race (Edinburgh, 1967), p. 124.

[6]Ibid., p. 51.

has been preparing the race, in foreign
lands, for a great work of grace on this
continent. The hand of God is on the
Black man in all the lands of his sojourn
for the good of Africa.[7]

Crummell was not the only Black American preacher who
felt this way during the latter nineteenth century
period. Bishop B.W. Arnett of the church founded by
anti-colonialist Richard Allen, organized a company
for trading with Africa in 1876, and favored the
selective emigration of Blacks with some capital
in order to help build up a New Christian Nationality
in the Fatherland, that would cause Blacks everywhere
to be respected.

The belief that Africa had a glorious past and
that the Black people of the New World were destined
to help "redeem it" and "regenerate it" lent powerful
impetus to the missionary movement of the Black
Methodist and Baptist Churches and to the Back-To-
Africa movements that arose from time to time. The
people involved believed that they were helping to
speed the day when "Princes shall come out of Egypt
and Ethiopia shall soon stretch forth her hand unto
God." Bishop Henry M. Turner of the African Methodist
Episcopal Church, in his outspoken and energetic style,
constantly called attention to the disadvantages of
the Black American; but nowhere has he given a more
vivid presentation of the dreary anddiscouraging
subject and the need for repatriation to Africa than
in an article in the Quarterly Review of his Church,
(The American Methodist Episcopal Church Review,
January, 1885). He wrote:

I need not repeat my well known convictions
as to the future of the race. I think
our stay in this country is but temporary,
at most. Nothing will remedy the evils
of the Negro, but a great Christian
nation upon the continent of Africa. White
is God in this country, and Black is the
Devil. White is perfection, greatness,
wisdom, industry, and all that is high and
holy. Black is ignorance, degradation,

---

[7]Ibid., p. 51

indolence, and all that is low and vile;
and three fourths of the colored people
of the land do nothing day and night but
cry: 'Glory, honor, dominion and greatness
to White.' Many of our so-called leading
men are contaminated with the accursed
disease or folly, as well as the thought-
less masses; and, as long as such a
sentiment pervades the colored race, the
powers of Heaven cannot elevate him. No
race of people can rise and manufacture
better conditions while they hate and
condemn themselves. A man must believe he
is somebody, before he is acknowledged to
be somebody. Hundreds of our most educated
young men will put on as many airs over a
position that requires them to dust the
clothes of white men, as a superior man
would over an appointment to the President's
Cabinet. I deny that God Himself could
make a great man out of such a character,
without a miracle.[8]

Bishop Turner was convinced that the Black man was
brought to the New World in the providence of God
'to learn obedience, to work, to sing, to pray, to
preach, acquire education, and imbibe the principles
of civilization as a whole, and then return to Africa.'
To give effect to his ideas he organized The Colored
Emigration and Commercial Association which had a
large following in some areas of rural South, but sent
no exiles home.

The great Black pioneers who pushed ardently in
the nineteenth century towards the objective of
African Zionism fervently believed that under the
united labors of the Black race, Africa could have
been reclaimed. They possessed an undying hope in
the future, and often eloquently attested to this
hope. At the close of the century, one such pioneer,
Edward Blyden proclaimed:

In visions of the future, I behold those
beautiful hills - the banks of those
charming streams, the verdant plains and

---

[8]Ibid., p. 353

flowery fields, the salubrious highlands
in primeval innocence and glory, and
those fertile districts watered everywhere as the garden of the Lord; I see
them all taken possession of by the
returning exiles from the West, trained
for the work of rebuilding waste places
under severe discipline and hard
bondage. I see, too, their brethren
hastening to welcome them from the
slopes of Niger, and from its lovely
valleys--from many a sequestered nook,
and from many, a palmy plain--Mohammedans
and Pagans, chiefs and people, all
coming to catch something of the
inspiration the exiles have brought--
to share in the borrowed jewels they
have imported, and to march back hand-
in-hand with their returned brethren
towards the sunrise for the regeneration
of a continent . . . "Ethiopia shall
suddenly stretch forth her hands unto
God."[9]

Blyden contended that the Black race had a duty to
perform in the history of human civilization, and
Africa was awaiting the return of the Black man
from the New World:

Let him be delirered from the restraints
of his exile; let him be set free from
the stocks that now confine him, and he
will not only arise and walk, but he
will point out the way to the eminent
success, which, in his particular life,
only he can find out, and which he must
find out for himself. He will discover
the central point from which the lines
may be easily and infallibly drawn to
all the points of the circle in which
he is to move effectively, in the true work
of his race, for his own elevation and
the advantage of the rest of mankind . . .

---

[9]Ibid., pp. 128-129.

> Let him then return to the land of his
> fathers, and acquaint himself with God,
> and be at peace.[10]

It is worth noting that Blyden made this appeal in
1887, the same year that Marcus Garvey was born. The
impact of this appeal by this Pan-African patriot must
have been felt later by Marcus Garvey, as he captured
this vision in the twentieth century, and adopted
it as the focus for his African Zionist movement -
the Universal Negro Improvement Association.

The nineteenth century came to a close with the
rise to prominence of another leading Black pioneer--
Booker T. Washington. In 1895 Booker T. Washington
made his epochal Atlanta speech outlining the doctrine
of industrial education for the Black race. There
was criticism by Dr. W.E.B. Du Bois and others who
felt that the doctrine of industrial education had
been interpreted as meaning that it was the only
education the Black race would need to fit it for the
place it was to occupy in society. There was also
criticism of the minimizing of political and civil
rights. However, over against these criticisms stood
the great, concrete demonstration, Tuskegee Institute
which was doing a tremendous work for the Blacks of
the South. The fact that he succeeded so far as he
did, notwithstanding the popular conception of him as
only an earnest educator and an energetic builder,
stamps him as one of the world's ablest diplomats.
The great body of the Blacks, discouraged, bewildered,
and leaderless, hailed Booker T. Washington as a Moses.
His ability tohold the South in one hand, the North
in the other, and at the same time carrying the major
portion of his race along with him was a remarkable
feat. This act of uniting these three factions in
the attempt to benefit the third had been tried before,
but never achieved. At the height of his career,
Booker T. Washington was by long odds the most
distinguished man the South had produced after the
era following that of the Civil War heroes. It was
in London that Garvey first read Booker T. Washington
Washington's autobiography, Up From Slavery which, by
his own confession had a profound effect upon him.

---

[10]Ibid., pp. 150-151.

An inspired Garvey returned to Jamaica on July 15, 1914 and launched the Universal Negro Improvement Association. That same year Garvey acaepted an invitation from his new hero to visit the United States, but Washington died before Garvey could set out. Garvey must have been influenced greatly by Washington. Consequently, on March 23, 1916 when Garvey arrived in Harlem, he was to discover a stage that was appropriate for his magnificent designs.

B. The Harlem Renaissance of the Early 20th Century

     At the beginning of the twentieth century, Dr.
W.E.B. Du Bois, a social scientist, historian and
pioneer in the Black liberation struggle--in the
United States and in Africa, put the Western World on
notice that the problem of the 20th century was the
problem of the color-line. Years later he wrote, with
even greater certainty:

> Most men in the world are colored. A
> belief in humanity means a belief in
> colored men. The future world will,
> in all reasonable possibility, be
> what colored men make it.[11]

It was at the first Pan-African Congress held in
London, July 1900, that the word "Pan-Africanism"
became a part of the universal language, and the
concept, itself, became a rallying point for the
African liberation movement. In a speech at that
Conference, Du Bois asserted the role of the Black
race in human civilization, and affirmed their inte-
grity in past history:

> In the metropolis of the modern world,
> in this the closing year of the nineteenth
> century, there has been assembled a
> congress of men and women of African blood,
> to deliberate solemnly upon the present
> situation and outlook of the darker races
> of mankind. The problem of the twentieth
> century is the problem of the color-line,
> the question as to how far differences of
> race--which show themselves chiefly in
> the color of the skin and the texture
> of the hair--will hereafter be made the
> basis of denying to over half the world
> the right of sharing to their utmost
> ability the opportunities and privileges
> of modern civilization. To be sure, the
> darker races are today the least advanced
> in culture according to European standards.

---

[11]W.E.B. Du Bois, An ABC of Color (New York,
1963), p. 11.

This has not, however, always been the
case in the past, and certainly the
world's history, both ancient and
modern, has given many instances of
no despicable ability and capacity among
the blackest races of men.[12]

The early years of the new century were for Dr.
Du Bois years of accomplishment, years of study, and
of political activity. It was the time when Black
Americans began to form their own organizations which
would combat discrimination. Dr. Du Bois was a
spokesman for this new movement, and found himself at
the head of the scattered and almost silent remnants
of the old militant Black element. In 1903 he wrote
a book entitled The Souls of Black Folk. This book
of his was at once hailed as a great book. It was a
collection of essays, one of which was headed "Of Mr.
Washington and Others" and contained an estimate of
Booker T. Washington and a statement of the points of
which the author differed with him. Du Bois came into
sharp criticism, especially from the South. But the
chief significance of this essay lies in the effect
wrought by it within the race. It brought about a
coalescence of the more radical elements and made
them articulate, as Du Bois stated in the essay:

The Black men of America have a duty to
perform, a duty stern and delicate--a
forward movement to oppose a part of
the work of their greatest leader. So
far as Mr. Washington preaches Trift,
Patience and Industrial Training for
the masses, we must hold up his hands
and strive with him, rejoicing in his
honors and glorying in the strength of
this Joshua called of God and of man
to lead the headless host. But so far
as Mr. Washington apologizes for injustice,
North or South, does not rightly value
the privilege and duty of voting, belittles
the emasculating effects of caste
distinctions, and opposes the higher
training and ambition of our brightest

---

[12]Ibid., pp. 20-21.

minds--so far as he, the South, or the
nation, does this--we must increasingly
and firmly oppose them.[13]

In an answer to a call sent out by him, a conference
was held, July 11-13, 1905, at Buffalo, New York.
Twenty-nine Black men were present from thirteen
states and the District of Columbia. Three states
of the Old South--Georgia, Tennessee, and Virginia--
were represented. A national organization was formed
and called "The Niagara Movement". The following
year, in August, the Niagara Movement met at Harper's
Ferry, the scene of John Brown's martyrdom, and
adopted and sent out An Address to The Country which,
in part, read:

> The men of the Niagara Movement coming
> from the toil of the year's hard work
> and pausing for a moment from the earning
> of their daily bread turn toward the
> nation and again ask in the name of ten
> million the privilege of a hearing. In
> the past year the work of the Negro
> hater has flourished in the land. Step
> by step the defenders of the rights of
> American citizens have retreated . . .
> Against this the Niagara Movement
> eternally protests. We will not be
> satisfied to take one jot or little less
> than our full manhood rights. We claim
> for ourselves every single right that
> belongs to a freeborn American, political,
> civil and social; and until we get these
> rights we will never cease to protest
> and assail the ears of America . . .[14]

In May 1910 a second conference was held, in New
York, at which there was consummated a merger of the
forces of the Black liberals of the Niagara Movement,
and the White liberals of abolition traditions, thus
forming the National Association for the Advancement

---

[13]Nathan Irvin Huggins, ed., Voices From The
Harlem Renaissance (New York, 1976), p. 62.

[14]Ibid., p. 61.

16

of Colored People. This was the first and only
organization since the Anti-Slavery Society providing
a common medium for the cooperation of Blacks and
Whites in the work of serving and safeguarding the
common citizenship rights of the Black American.
With the founding of this association New York became
again the center of the organized forces of self-
assertion of equal rights and of insistence upon the
impartial application of the fundamental principles
of the Republic, without regard to race, creed, or
color.

Shortly following the formation of the NAACP
steps were taken which led to the establishment of
another important national organization to work for
the Black people, with headquarters in New York, the
National Urban League on urban conditions among
Blacks. The main purpose for which this organization
was formed was to work for the industrial, social,
and health betterment of the Black people, especially
those living in urban centers. In additions to
working for these ends, the Urban League has carried
on research work and collected a great deal of
valuable data and statistics on industrial, social,
and health conditions among Blacks. Both races
cooperated in the Urban League.

Ten years after the forming of these two bodies
another organization, destined to create among Blacks
pride, confidence, and cultural identity, was in full
swing in Harlem. This organization, the Universal
Negro Improvement Association, founded by Marcus
Garvey, excited the imagination and stirred the
enthusiasm of the entire Harlem community. In 1920
Garvey staged the first Universal Negro Convention in
Harlem. This was the dramatic occasion that made the
city of New York fully aware of the movement in Harlem.
If Marcus Garvey did not originate the phrase, the New
Negro, he at least made it popular.

The flowering of the Harlem's creative life came
in the Garvey era. The Anthology, The New Negro,
which orientated the debut of the Renaissance writers,
was printed in 1925 when Alain Locke, a professor of
philosophy at Howard University brought out a
collection of essays, stories, and poetry. His
introductory essay served to redefine the "New Negro"
in cultural terms, almost ignoring the political
emphasis of a decade earlier. In announcing the
arrival of the New Negro on the Harlem scene, Alain

Locke wrote:

> In the last decade something beyond the
> watch and guard of statistics has happened
> in the life of the American Negro and the
> three norms who have traditionally presided
> over the Negro problem have a changeling
> in their laps. The Sociologist, the
> Philanthropist, the Race-Leader are not
> unaware of the New Negro, but they are
> at a loss to account for him. He simply
> cannot be swathed in their formulas. For
> the younger generation is vibrant with
> a new psychology; the new spirit is
> awake in the masses, and under the very
> eyes of the professional observers is
> transforming what has been a perennial
> problem into the progressive phases of
> contemporary Negro life.
>
> Could such a metamorphasis have taken place
> as suddenly as it has appeared to? The
> answer is no; not because the Old Negro
> had long become more of a myth than a
> man.[15]

Those Black Americans who were part of that decade of
change--roughly between World War I and the Great
Depression--saw themselves as principals in that
moment of transformation from the old to the new.
Thus, for them the expression "New Negro" told the
world of their self-concept. They characterized this
"New Negro", this new man, as having shed the costume
of the shuffling darky, the uncle and aunty, the sub-
servient and docile retainer, the clown. He was,
rather, a man and a citizen in his own right--
intelligent, articulate, self-assured. The "New
Negro" was telling all Americans that it was a new
day, and that he was a revived and inspired
competitor. No longer could he be dismissed by
contempt, pity, or terror. He would insist upon his
rights, and if necessary, return violence, blow for
blow. It was all suggestive of the shift in sentiment from the leadership of Booker T. Washington to

---

[15]Ibid., p. 47.

18

that of W.E.B. Du Bois, and later to Marcus Garvey.
The "New Negro" intended to define himself in new
terms, outside the convenient stereotype. The
audience, black and white, could take it or leave it.

There was a confluence of forces that created the
atmosphere in which the Harlem Renaissance developed.
The urganization of American Society created the fact
of Harlem, and brought changes in assumptions and
habits of life that transformed both White and Black
Americans into new people. Harlem was America's
cultural capital, open to cross-currents from around
the world! Blacks were coming to the city not only
from the South but also from the French and British
West Indies, including Marcus Garvey from Jamaica,
and Africa. There was a cross-fertilization of Black
intelligence and culture as in no other place in the
world. At the same moment, Blacks from the British
empire were using London as their stage for promoting
their futures. And others from Martinique, Haiti,
and Senegal were delivering manifestoes from Paris.
It would seem that the entire world of Black people
was in ferment. The Harlem Renaissance was thus not
isolated but part of a world-wide phenomenon. It was
also part of a process that had been well underway by
the opening of the 1920's. Whether in the studied
language of W.E.B. Du Bois or in the more flamboyant
rhetoric of Marcus Garvey, these Black leaders were
announcing a strikingly new independence for Black
Americans. Garvey responded to the theological
question that arose out of this Harlem context: "Could
those forces which had sustained Black American
culture--notably the Christian Church--be relied on as
a continuing inspiration for the New Negro?" It was
during this period that Garvey broke away from the
Roman Catholic Church and launched out in a new field.
He established the African Orthodox Church as an
adjunct to his organization, and appointed the
Reverend George McGuire, a minister of the Episcopalian Church as the Archbishop. This was a bold
stroke which excited the imagination of his followers.
They would have their own church.

A very important part of the thought and
expression of the Harlem Renaissance, in both its
religious and cultural forms, had to do with the
finding of comfortable emotional and intellectual
accomodation of Black Americans to their African
origins. Thus, it is a question of identity which
underlies Alain Locke's essay on African art, just as

19

it does much of the poetry of Countee Cullen, Langston Hughes and Claude McKay. Africa could not be discussed with academic distance. Even Du Bois, writing in his diary off the coast of Africa, tells us that his was no mere pleasure trip but a journey to find some part of himself. The question about Africa was asked in many ways; the answer merely fed the enigma. The Harlem Renaissance, however, brought the question to a high level of consciousness among Black people. Even with the rude transplanting of slavery, that uprooted the technical elements of their former culture, Black Americans brought over as an emotional inheritance a deep seated aesthetic endowment. This offshoot of the African spirit blended itself in with entirely different culture elements and blossomed in strange new forms.

The innumerable cults, mystic chapels, and occult shops which abound in Harlem are explainable only by tracing back to the original African roots. "Millions of natives may come under the sway of either of the great rival religions of Islam and Christianity, but it is on pagan terms. Their profession of faith is pervaded by occult imagery. The fetish gods rule their hearts and the secret ritual of jungle magic is evoked to appease the obscure yearnings of the mind, which civilized religion cannot satisfy." (See Ben-Jochannan, African Origins of Western Religious).[16] Whether they are West Indian or Southern practitioners of the occult science in Harlem, their ritual is basically similar in form and style to the performance of the Guinea fetishers. In Harlem they have refined their work and enlarged their scope. Strange cults have always been numerous in Harlem. The Black Church has gone a long way towards letting its people go to the extreme of spiritual license. But the church is no adequate outlet for the burning religious energy of the Black masses. Therefore, the cults multiply in Harlem. They are the spiritual spice of the Harlem scene. Yet it is because the Harlem Renaissance seems so seminal and symbolic of the Black American coming of age that it will always awaken in Black Americans a sense of personal trial and achievement.

---

[16]Yosef Ben-Jochannan, African Origins of The Major Western Religions (New York, 1970), p. 175.

The poet Claude McKay captured this sense of trial
and achievement in his poem entitled, If We Must Die:

> If we must die, let it not be like hogs
> Hunted and penned in an inglorious spot,
> While round us bark the made and hungry
> dogs, Making their mock at our accursed
> lot. If we must die, O let us nobly die,
> So that our precious blood may not be shed
> In vain; then even the monsters we defy
> Shall be contrained to honor us though
> dead! Okinsmen! We must meet the common
> doe! Though far outnumbered let us show
> us brave And for their thousand blows
> deal one death blow; What though before
> us lies the open grave? Like men we'll
> face the murderous, cowardly pack, Pressed
> to the wall, dying but fighting back![17]

A similar note is found in Countee Cullen's From the
Dark Tower:

> We shall not always plant while other reap
> The golden increment of bursting fruit,
> Not always countenance, object and mute,
> That lesser men should hold their brothers
> cheap; Not everlastingly while others
> sleep Shall we beguile their limbs with
> mellow flute, Not always bend to some more
> subtle brute; We were not made eternally
> to weep.
>
> The night whose sable breast relieves the
> stark, White stars is no less lovely being
> dark, And there are buds that cannot bloom
> at all In light, but crumple, piteous,
> and fall; So in the dark we hide the heart
> that bleeds, And wait, and tend our
> agonizing seeds.[18]

The Harlem Renaissance period is indeed a historical
watershed in the Black experience. Harlem provided

---

[17]Huggins, Voices From the Harlem Renaissance,
pp. 353-354.

[18]Ibid., p. 360.

a seed-bed for Marcus Garvey. He came like the Black
Moses to create among Blacks, long demoralized in a
contemptuous white-deominated society, pride, confidence, and a cultural identity, by assigning them
a special and significant role. He came with an
appeal "Up You Mighty Race!"

Chapter II

MARCUS GARVEY: THE MAN AND THE MOVEMENT

> We are men; we have souls, we have
> passions, We have feelings, we have
> hopes, We have desires, like any other
> race in the world. The cry is raised
> allover the world today of Canada for
> the Canadians, of America for the
> Americans, of England for the English,
> of France for the French, of Germany
> for the Germans--Do you think it
> unreasonable that we, the Blacks of
> the world, should raise the cry of
> Africa for the Africans?[1]

Thus spoke Marcus Garvey, the architect of the
African Zionist Movement and one of the greatest mass
leaders of Black Americans. He came to his Race
endowed with an extraordinary capacity for
organization and leadership, and an undaunted faith
in the possibilities of his people. Garvey's
spiritual enthusiasm was not a program of consolation
through emotional and spiritual complacency. He
led the way in mass organization of Blacks. He
blazed the trail in militancy. He sacrificed his
freedom in one mighty effort to give to Blacks a
higher emancipation--both spiritual and human.

Marcus Mosiah Garvey was born on the 17th of
August, 1887 to Marcus and Sarah Garvey in Jamaica,
an island in the Caribbean. His father is said to
have been a descendant of the maroons--these were
Africans who, having fled to the hills to establish
free communities after the English had captured
Jamaica from the Spaniards in 1655, successfully
combatted several British military attacks. In
1739 these Maroons gained local autonomy from the
White rulers of Jamaica. Marcus Garvey in his
youth must have heard the stories of great Maroon
heroes such as Quaco, Cudjoe and Champong Mannie,
as well as those Three-Finger Jack, Paul Bogle and

---

[1]Marcus Garvey, "Speech Presenting The Case of
The Negro For International Racial Adjustment"
(London, 1928), p. 1.

and William Gordon, all of them the honored heroes of the Black man's struggle against White enslavement. He grew up knowing that his father bore the proud Ashanti blood in his veins. His mother was quite the opposite. She was a soft-hearted, conscientious Christian woman.

From this union, eleven children were brought forth, but all died in childhood, except Marcus and a sister, Indiana. His father believed in planetary influences and upon giving him the name Marcus said that 'any boy born under the planet Leo--the Lion, when the Sun is in the ascendancy, is bound to be a leader in his line.' His mother wanted to name him Moses, hoping that he would be like Moses and lead his people. A compromise was struck, and he was given as a middle name, Mosiah. He grew up very close to his mother, while his father spent most of his time reading and brooding.

In Jamaica, young Garvey spent his youth like most Jamaicans, playing with other boys and girls in his neighborhood, paying no attention to color. The Whites in St. Ann's Bay were mainly children of missionaries and landed gentry, but he never seemed to note the difference until he was fourteen years old. The incident that brought this new awareness was the departure for England of the white minister's daughter with whom he had a boyhood relationship. She was told not to keep in touch with Garvey because he was a "nigger." Garvey never forgot this incident. He began to observe Jamaican society and was disturbed at the privilege shown to boys of white or near-white parentage. They were given preparation for government posts, being sent either to the few prestigious schools in Jamaica or to England to study. In contrast, the blacker boys were given menial trades as laborers on the large plantations, or in a few cases, when they were especially bright, they became teachers in government and private schools.

At fourteen young Garvey had to leave elementary school and became an apprentice in a small country printshop owned by his god-father. As a boy, Marcus Garvey was strong-willed. He hated defeat and as he later said in his autobiography:

> It annoys me to be defeated;
> Hence to me, to be once defeated
> is to find cause for an everlasting

24

struggle to reach the top.[2]

Thus when he went into the printing trade, he naturally went on to become one of the best in that business, and took a job as a printer in the city. Garvey was also determined to be a good speaker. Every Sunday he visited different churches to get pointers in platform deportment and oratory from the preachers. Many evenings he and others used to have discussion groups on all sorts of subjects. At home he practiced various gestures in front of the mirror while reading from schoolbooks, and became so advanced in oratory that he organized the first class in elocution in Kingston, Jamaica. This training was to be invaluable for his success as a Black leader. However, what was uppermost in his mind was how to improve the lot of the poor working people. Thus he helped to form the first political club in Jamaica--the National Club--which issued a publication fortnightly called Our Own.

In 1910, Garvey who was becoming by now increasingly restless started a periodical, the Garvey's Watchman, which proved an unsuccessful venture. He then left for Costa Rica, and was terribly disturbed by the plight of the Black workers in the United Fruit Company's Plantations. He was now more determined to work for the improvement of the lot of the masses of his race wherever they may be. He was convinced that no White man would ever regard the life of a Black man equal to that of a White man. Again he started another paper called La Nacionale.

Garvey returned to Jamica in 1911, tried to enlist the support of the Jamaican government, but found that the British officials there were as equally indifferent to the plight of the Blacks. In 1912 when Garvey found himself in a position to travel, he decided to observe the conditions of the Black man in other parts of the West Indies and in South America. He later visited England as well. In these countries he found that the same conditions of deprivation and disenfranchisement prevailed

---

[2]Amy Jacques-Garvey, Philosophy of Opinions of Marcus Garvey (New York, 1977), II, p. 124.

among the Blacks. In England, he learned about Africa and its people, its ancient history and its economic potential. He immediately made contacts with African and West Indian Nationalists, students and seamen, and became deeply agitated by the colonial question, especially as it affected his African "Fatherland." The call suddenly seized him and in his own words he recorded his experience as follows:

> I went travelling in South America and other parts of the West Indies to find out if it was so elsewhere, and found the same situation. I set sail for Europe to find out if it were different there, and again I found the stumbling block--"You are Black." I read the conditions in America. I read Up From Slavery by Booker T. Washington . . . I asked: "Where is the Black man's king and kingdom?" "Where is his President, his country, his ambassador, his army, his navy, his men of big affairs?" I could not find them and I declared, I will help to make them.[3]

Garvey was traumatically struck by the deteriorated position of the Black people throughout the world. He continued:

> My young and ambitious mind led me into flights of great imagination. I saw before me then, as I do now, a new world of Black men, not peons, serfs, dogs and slaves, but a nation of sturdy men making their impress upon civilization and causing a new light to dawn upon the human race . . . My brain was afire. There was a world of thought to conquer. I had to start ere it became too late and the work be not done.[4]

---

[3]Ibid., p. 126.

[4]Ibid., p. 126.

Here then, in London, in 1912, it seemed destined that one of the sons of the Black Diaspora should spearhead the struggle for the redemption of Africa, and foster unity with those abroad and at home. Garvey was twenty-seven years of age and had developed a keen interest in the revival of the human spirit in Black people.

Garvey left England in the summer of 1914 inspired with the idea of uniting all the Black people of the world into one great body to establish a country and government absolutely their own. Five days after arriving in Jamaica he established the Universal Negro Improvement Association and African Communities League, and invited all the Black people, or "persons of Negro or African parentage" to join him in the crusade for rehabilitation of the race. The name of the movement had been revealed to Garvey in a vision, as he stated:

> At midnight, lying flat on my back, the vision and thought came to me that I should name the organization the Universal Negro Improvement Association and African Communities League. Such a name I thought would embrace the purpose of all Black humanity. Thus to the world a name was born, a movement created, a man became known.[5]

Garvey became the President. Between 1914 and 1916 Garvey labored to unite the Black masses in Jamaica and to educate the "Black bourgeoisie" to appreciate their responsibility towards the proletarians among the race. The effort was largely unsuccessful, partly because of hostility, and partly because of the apathy of the masses.

In the meantime, with the nucleus of the Jamaican movement established, Garvey, the man of undaunted courage, began to look about for ways and means to extend his vision and broaden his organization. His thoughts turned to the United States, to the man whose work he greatly admired, Booker T. Washington, who was then at Tuskegee Institute in

---

[5]Ibid., p. 128.

Alabama. In 1915, Garvey wrote to Washington who encourage him to visit Tuskegee. However, he arrived in the United States in March 1916, and by that time Washington had died. In a sense Garvey filled the vacuum left by Booker T. Washington, and became subjected to an attack by Dr. W.E.B. Du Bois and the Black intelligentsia who were members of the NAACP. Thus intense leadership rivalry developed between spokesmen of the Black elite and Garvey. His arrival in New York City was most auspicious, for the death of Washington, the great compromiser, had left the mass of American Blacks without a leader. The few intellectual Blacks had become more and more disenchanted with the "Tuskegee Machine" anyway and had vigorously denounced the leadership of Washington. Yet there was no Black intellectual really capable of controlling and using the great tide of social change about to sweep the American scene. Between the years 1916 and 1918 over half a million Southern Blacks had moved North in search of better jobs and living conditions. During those same years Garvey traveled through several United States cities exciting audiences. By 1919 he had traveled across thirty-eight states.

Garvey established a brance of the Universal Negro Improvement Association in Harlem in 1917. In two months, he built up a new organization of about 1,500 members. Five years later the membership had increased to "several" million Blakcs in the United States, the West Indies, Latin America, and Africa. Indeed Garvey was regarded as a Pan-African Nationalist. In 1918 he published the Negro World, a journal that carried the story of Garvey and his movement across the world. It was printed in several languages. In 1919 Garvey launched the Black Star Shipping Line to link Blacks across the world. He then sent a group of technicians to Liberia, Africa and launched a two million dollars loan to rehabilitate Liberia. In that same year he purchased an auditorium of a Harlem church and renamed it Liberty Hall. It was there in 1920 that the First International Convention was held.

In 1921 Garvey organized the African Orthodox Church as an adjunct to the UNIA, and appointed Reverend George McGuire, an Episcopalian priest, as Archbishop. From this platform, Garvey expounded his theology which included a multi-facial heaven,

Christ embodying all races, a Negro God, and
replaced portraits of a White Christ and White
Madonna and child with Black figures.

In 1922, Garvey was arrested on a charge of
using the mail to defraud. He risked his honor and
the movement on a highly competitive shipping
business, and was convicted and sentenced to prison.
It is very difficult to resist the conclusion that
Garvey's conviction was political. In 1927, his
sentence was commuted by President Coolidge and he
was deported to Jamaica as an undesirable alien.
He continued his work in Jamaica, and in 1928 he and
his wife traveled to Europe where he established
UNIA branches in London and Paris, and presented
a petition to the League of Nations in Geneva.

Garvey called the Sixth International Convention
in Jamaica in 1919. This was the last great UNIA
Convention. In that same year he was elected to a
seat in the City Council in Kingston, Jamaica. In
1930 he campaigned unsuccessfully for the Legislature,
and his organization began to decline and disinte-
grate in Jamaica. In 1935 he moved his headquarters
from Kingston, Jamaica to London. During the years
1936, 1937 and 1938, Garvey presided over UNIA
Conventions in Toronto, Canada. Garvey spent his
remaining years in London where he died on June 10,
1940.

If one can count those millions who were inspired
by Garvey, and thus changed their attitude towards
life, and their way of life, then, you can count
Garveyites all over the world--then and now. First
of all, then:

> Outsiders will never understand the
> psychology of those they call Garveyites.
> We doubt if we who are thus nicknamed
> understand it ourselves. The binding
> spell, the indefinable charm which Mr.
> Garvey exercises over us beggars
> description. But we find reason for it
> in our conviction that no man has spoken
> to us like this man, inculcating pride
> and nobility of race, and clearly
> pointing out the Star of Hope to a

discouraged and downtrodden people.[6]

and second, now:

> Today, we once again honor the memory of
> the late Marcus Garvey, a national and
> international hero--a Black man who
> dedicated his life and existence to
> unifying Africans and people of
> African descent. His goal was to
> provide Blacks with the economic
> ability to become a force to be
> reckoned with. He recognized that to
> be truly free, the Black man had to have
> control of his own economic situation . . .
> our commitment is therefore to ourselves,
> as African descendants, and to Mother
> Africa. Our commitment is especially
> to our Black youth who will inherit our
> victories and our defeats. We must
> ensure that the victories heavily
> outweight the defeats. So we call for
> peace among Blacks first. A brotherhood,
> a unity. A singlemindedness of purpose.
> A common bond to put Africa and the Black
> man above all else. As Blacks we were
> truly set upon the right path when Marcus
> Garvey stated his philosophy--so boldly,
> yet so profoundly--"One God, One Aim, One
> Destiny."[7]

If Garvey was not inspired as a servant of his
race, he could not, and would not have suffered all
he did daily. What happened to Marcus Garvey was
nothing compared to what was happening to millions of
his people everywhere. Garvey must have been inspired
to have been so persevering in his ideas and actions.
Garvey, the man, is dead; but the movement and the
message live on.

---

[6]Amy Jacques-Garvey, Garvey and Garveyism
(London, 1970), p. 325.

[7](Part of a text delivered by James R. Lawson,
on Thursday, 17th August, 1978 in Kingston, Jamaica,
during the Annual Convention of the UNIA held at
National Heroes Park, commemorating the birthday of
Marcus Garvey.)

In commemorating Garvey's birthday, a Jamaican journalist and news analyst, Frank Hill, wrote under the heading "The Prophet of Black Zionism":

> What makes a man great? It is, I think, the universal quality of the contribution he makes to the civilization of his times. The accent is on the word universal, for the quality of his vision must be of such as to be able to hold the attention of mankind, rather than mere isolated pockets of men grouped in special circumstances . . .
>
> What was the significance of Garvey? The Prophet of Black Zionism beat the drums for the in-gathering to Africa. He may have meant it as a summons for a physical recall. But the message went more deeply, more enduringly than that. Eyes and hearts and minds turned to Africa—to the new values and standards and principles that earned their validity from the culture that grew out of the African Community.[8]

The ideas of Garvey and the Garvey movement live on in the spirit of the Black movements of today, in some cases as the original inspirations of lesser revolutionaries, and in other cases as the substance of the ideals and aspirations of Black people in general.

---

[8](Article in the Daily Gleaner, August 17, 1960, under the heading "The Prophet of Black Zionism").

Chapter III

Garvey's Philosophy of History

The object of Garvey was to creat among Blacks
long demoralized in a contemptuous white dominated
world, pride, confidence and a cultural identity by
assigning them a special and significant role in
history. It is therefore necessary to understand
and grasp Garvey's philosophy of history in order
to identify the context out of which this role would
become operative. It was Garvey's view that history
is the land-mark by which we are directed into the
true course of life. He related the role of Black
people to the sweep of human civilization as a whole.
In an analysis of the present day civilization he
noted that:

> We are circumvented today by environments
> more dangerous than those which circumvented
> other peoples in any other age. We are
> face to face with environments in a
> civilization that is highly developed;
> a civilization that is competing with
> itself for its own destruction; a
> civilization that cannot last, because
> it has no spiritual foundation; a
> civilization that is vicious, crafty,
> dishonest, immoral, irreligious and
> corrupt.
>
> As by indication, the fall will come. A
> fall that will cause the universal wreck
> of the civilization that we now see, and
> in this civilization the Negro is called
> upon to play his part. He is called
> upon to evolve a national ideal, based
> upon freedom, human liberty and true
> democracy.[1]

He was convinced that no race or people can well
survive with an aim or purpose, and challenged
Blacks to know beforehand the purpose of their existence, and to move forward to unite the race the world

---

[1]Garvey, Philosophy of Opinion, I, p. 31.

over:

> Go ahead, Negroes, and organize
> yourselves! You are serving your
> race and guaranteeing to posterity
> of our own an existence which other-
> wise will be denied them. To suggest
> that there is no need for Negro racial
> organization in a well-planned and
> arranged civilization like that of
> the twentieth century is but to, by
> the game of deception, lay the trap
> for the destruction of a people whose
> knowledge of life is incomplete, owing
> to their misunderstanding of man's
> purpose in creation.[2]

In order to provide a base for this major thrust of
racial organization Garvey pointed to an exemplar
in history--primitive African civilization. With
this backdrop he also raised the questions: 'Where
is the Black man's King and Kingdom? Where is his
President, his country, his ambassador, his army,
his navy, his men of big affairs?'

As one studies the various racially organized
groups in history, one cannot fail to come to grips
with the fact that the thrust seems to be centered
around questions raised by human beings within a
particular historical context, whether it be
cultural or religious, social or political. In his
Prolegomena to the History of Primitivism, the
philosopher/historian, Arthur O. Lovejoy presented
the context in which the answers to these questions
are located. He referred to this context as
"primitivism," and distinguished two tendencies
thereof--one he called "chronological," and the
other "cultural" primitivism. In describing
chronological primitivism, Lovejoy stated:

> Chronological primitivism is one of many
> answers which may be and have been given
> to the question: What is the temporal
> distribution of good, or value, in the
> history of mankind, or more generally,

---

[2]Ibid., p. 16.

in the entire history of the world.[3]

With regards, cultural primitivism, he stated:

> Cultural primitivism is the discontent
> of the civilized with civilization, or
> with some conspicuous and characteristic
> feature of it. It is the belief of men
> living in a relatively highly evolved and
> complex cultural condition that a life
> far simpler and less sophisticated in
> some or in all respects is a more
> desirable life.[4]

Lovejoy also asserted that the two forms of
"primitivism" can be fused or can remain disassociated
from each other. In terms of Garvey's philosophy of
history, we will recognize a similar fusion in that
he not only enunciated an ideal in his theory of
racial organization, but he also pointed to an
exemplar in history--Africa. This mode of thinking
was also referred to as "Ethiopianism." If we
substitute Lovejoy's concept of "primitivism" for
Garvey's theory of "Ethiopianism" we find a striking
similarity in their ideas. Lovejoy recognized that
in the study of primitivism there is a tendency for
some organized groups to envision the pinnacle, the
source of salvation somewhere in the past, and to
see it again as a chance for the present. In
similar fashion, Garvey advocated the organization
of the NeGro Race from the historical perspective
of the history of man, and more particularly from
the history of a previous civilization in Africa
when Negroes were once a mighty race:

> When we come to consider the history of
> man, was not the Negro a power, was he
> not great once? Yes, honest students of
> history can recall the day when Egypt,
> Ethiopia and Timbuctoo towered in their
> civilizations, towered about Europe,

---

[3]Arthur Lovejoy, Prolegomena to the History of
Primitivism, p. 1.

[4]Ibid., p. 7.

towered above Asia. When Europe was
inhabited by a race of cannibals, a race
of savages, maked men, heathens and pagans.
Africa was peopled with a race of cultured
black men, who were masters in art, science,
and literature; men who were cultured and
refined; men who, it was said, were like
the gods. Even the great poets of old
sang in beautiful sonnets of the delight,
it afforded the gods to be in companionship
with Ethiopians. Why, then should we lose
hope? Black men, you were once great;
you shall be great again. Lose not
courage, lose not faith, go forward. The
thing to do is to get organized; keep
separated and you will be exploited, you
will be robbed, you will be killed. Get
organized, and you will compel the world to
respect you.[5]

But Garvey was also inspired by a vision of the future
in which he pictured a redeemed Africa:

So Negroes, I say, through the Universal
Negro Improvement Association, that
there is much to live for. I have a
vision of the future, and I see before
me a picture of a redeemed Africa, with
here dotted cities, with her beautiful
civilization, with her millions of happy
children, going to and fro. Why should
I lose hope, why should I give up and
take a back place in this age of progress? Remember that you are men, that
God created you Lords of this creation.
Lift up yourselves, men, take yourselves
out of the mire and hitch your hopes to
the stars; yes, rise as high as the very
stars themselves. Let no man pull you
down, let no man destroy your ambition,
because man is but your companion, your
equal; man is your brother; he is not

---

[5]Nathan Irvin Huggins, ed., Voices From
Harlem (New York, 1976), p. 41.

your lord; he is not your sovereign
master.[6]

Garvey's philosophy of history stemmed partly from
his deeply religious nature, in which he believed
and advocated the inscrutable working of a Divine
Providence for the ultimate good of the Negro Race,
and was partly a convenient rational for the unhappy
lot of his race. It possessed the supreme advantage
of being able, theoretically at least, to solve the
suffering and humiliation of the Negro Race in the
present by pointing to Negro achievements in Africa.
But more than this, it was intended to spur the race
to future greatness. Garvey contended that if Negroes
had in the past made outstanding contributions to
civilization, there was no reason why they should
not be able to do so in the future.

The central premise of this philosophy of
history can be characterized as a vision of the
whole, a monumental view of history, with the present
age regarded as a fixed point in the total process.
Invariably the present is seen as a crisis, a crucial
stage of transition. In this regards Garvey differed
from his predecessor Edward Blyden, the historical
progenitor of Pan-Africanism, who also expected
Blacks to take concerted action to help accelerate
'the divine plan' of bringing glory to the Black
Race, but who believed that the ultimate goal of
a nation or race was to serve humanity at large.

Blyden expressed this view of service in a
lecture delivered in Freetown Sierra, Leone in 1895
on 'Race and Study':

> For everyone of you--for everyone of us--
> there is a special work to be done--
> a work of tremendous importance--a work
> for the Race to which we belong . . .
> there is a responsibility which our
> personality, which our membership in
> the Race involves . . . the duty of
> every man, of every race is to contend
> for its individuality--to keep and
> develop it . . . Therefore, honour
> and love your Race. Be yourselves . . .
> If you are not yourself, if you
> surrender your personality, you have
> nothing left to give the world. You
> have no pleasure, no use, nothing

which will attract and charm me,
for by the suppression of your
individuality, you lose your
distinctive character . . . You
will see, then, that to give up
our personality, would be to give
up the peculiar work and glory to
which we are called. It would
really be to give up the divine
idea--to give up God--to sacrifice
the divine individuality; and this
is the worst of suicides.[7]

But what, in Blyden's view, were the distinctive
attributes of the Negro Race, what were the special
contributions it could make to civilization? In so
far as he attempted to determine this, Blyden was
obviously influenced by the historical circumstances
of the Negro race, as well as by certain aspects of
contemporary nationalist ideas. Blyden portrayed
his African as the antithesis of the European, and
serving to counteract the worst aspects of the
influence of the latter. The European character,
according to Blyden, was harsh, individualistic,
competitive and combative. European society was
highly materialistic: the worship of science and
industry was replacing that of God. In the character
of the African, declared Blyden, was to be found
'the softer aspects of human nature; 'cheerfulness,
sympathy, willingness to serve, were some of its
marked attributes. The special contribution of
the African to civilization would be a spiritual
one--the spiritual conservatory of the world.
Blyden's philosophy of history took the firm of a
theocratic determinism. To Blyden, every reverse,
every disaster, every set-back of the Negro Race
was merely God's inscrutable unfolding of the
divine plan. He expressed this view with eloquence
and pathos in a sermon delivered in Boston in 1882:

They (Negroes) were to remember that
if they were despised and scorned, a
far greater than themselves had had
a similar experience. Christ was

---

[7]Lecture delivered in Freetown Sierra Leone on
'Race and Study', "Sierra Leone Times", (27 May 1893)

to be held up to the suffering
African . . . as a blessed illustration
of the glorious fact that persecution
and suffering and contempt are no
proof that God is not the loving father
of a people--but may be rather an
evidence of nearness to God seeing
that they have been chosen to tread
in the footsteps of the first born
of the creation, sufferings for the
welfare of others . . . All the
advancement made to a better future,
by individuals or race, has been made
through paths marked by suffering.
This great law is written not only in
the Bible, but upon all history.[8]

Blyden advanced the claim that the lot of Africa
resembled also His who made Himself of no reputation,
but took upon Himself the form of a servant, and,
having been made perfect through suffering, became
the 'captain of our salvation'. He further contended
that if the principle laid down by Christ is that by
which things are decided above, namely, that he who
would be chief must become the servant of all, then
we see the position which Africa and the Africans
must ultimately occupy. We must admit that through
serving man, Africa--Ethiopia--has been stretching
out her hands unto God. Of course, the main
difficulty in subscribing to theocratic determinism
as a philosophy of history lies with the interpretation of the Divine Plan. In that sense both Blyden
and Garvey differed in their use of the concept of
'Ethiopianism' as a part of the Providential Design
of God for the Negro Race.

Unlike Blyden's view of the Negro Race as
destined to serve humanity at large, Garvey argued
that Negroes should organize themselves to serve
their race and guarantee to posterity of their own
an existence which otherwise will be denied them.
He contended that to suggest that there is no need
for Negro racial organization in a well-planned and
arranged civilization like that of the twentieth

8"African Repository", LX, January 1884, p.11.

century is but to, by the game of deception, lay the
trap for the destruction of a people whose knowledge of life is incomplete, owing to their misunder-
standing of man's purpose in creation, and to ignore
the trend of human effort in the direction of self-
preservation:

> The Negro surrounded as he is, has no
> other alternative than going forward
> in the atmosphere of racial self-
> interest, working for the generation
> of the present and providing for
> those of our posterity. In the service
> of race the Universal Negro Improvement
> Association finds its program, and for
> its advocacy or promotion we offer
> no apology.[9]

Garvey viewed the plight of the Negro Race in the
light of twentieth century amterialism:

> It is true that twentieth century
> materialism has so scattered the interests
> of races and nations that the reali-
> zation of human ideals becomes more
> remote, but we dare not sink or destroy
> holy principles because of the wanton-
> ness and soullessness of our age. Time
> cannot save itself; it is for us to save
> and redeem Time; hence, the work that
> lies before us is not so much to
> identify ourselves with the scattered
> purpose and greed of others, but to
> create for ourselves a central ideal
> and make our lives conform to it in the
> singling out of a racial life that shall
> know no end.[10]

But Garvey also acknowledged in his philosophy of
history a theocratic determinism that underscored the

---

[9]Garvey, Philosophy of Opinions, I, p. 16.

[10]Ibid., p. 15.

inscrutable working of a Divine Plan for the ultimate good of the Negro Race. However, he interpreted this Divine Plan not as a commission to the Negro Race to serve the larger humanity but as God's call for the Negro Race to organize itself in the atmosphere of racial self-interest and for the sake of posterity. This interpretation by Garvey is also very much rooted in his theology of the goodness and glory of God's creation of the Negro Race:

> The man or woman who has no confidence in self is na unfortunate being, and is really a misfit in creation. God almighty created each and everyone of us for a place in the world, and for the least of us to think that we were created only to be what we are and not what we can make ourselves, is to impute an improper motive to the Creator for creating us.
>
> God Almighty created us all to be free. That the Negro race became a race of slaves was not the fault of God Almighty, the Divine Master, it was the fault of the race. Sloth, meglect, indifference, caused us to be slaves. Confidence, conviction, action will cause us to be free men today.[11]

Garvey did not dwell on the concept of a chosen people, an elect group, portrayed as a suffering people destined to serve other racial groups. Instead, Garvey affirmed the Negro Race as a people of God's creation, a God of Equality, created in His image and having an honored and equal place in the process of human history. He asserted that within the Negro is a sovereign power, an authority that is absolute, and challenged the Negro Race to organize itself into a new race, irrespective of what the world thinks:

> It is foolish for us to believe that the world can settle itself on chance. It is for man and God to settle the world. God acts indifferently and

---

11Ibid., p. 37.

His plan and purpose is generally
worked out through the agency of
human action. In His directed,
inspired prophecy He promised that
Ethiopia's day would come, not by
the world changing toward us, but
by our stretching out our hands unto
God. It doesn't mean the mere
physical test, but the universal
and independent effort to surround
ourselves with the full glory of man.[12]

Garvey strove for a united, emancipated and
improved Negro Race. His philosophy of history was
that expected of a race patriot in that it portrayed
the assertion of the role of the Negro Race in human
history. However, Garvey's philosophy of history
was undergirded by his theological understanding
of the purpose of God's creation of the Negro Race
in history, coupled with his consciousness of their
historical roots. Garvey saw the need for a
spiritual and cultural rejuvenation among the Negro
Race, and led the way in a mass organization of
his people. He sacrificed his freedom in one
mighty effort to give to the Negro Race a higher
emancipation--both spiritual and human, by awakening
in them a consciousness of historical continuity
with their homeland Africa:

Personally, I am glad to suffer for the
cause. My contribution to the race and
to Africa is small, but it is gladly
given without any regrets. Some of us
will contribute through our ability
and our lives, others through service
of other kind; but whatever it be, let
us give it freely. Do not falter or
faint by the wayside, but let us, with
confidence in ourselves and our God go
forth in the call for service to our
race and to Ethiopia.[13]

---

[12]Ibid., p. 16.

[13]Ibid., p. 17.

Garvey saw the role of the Negro Race in history as working towards the one glorious end of a free, redeemed and mighty nation:

> Let Africa be our guiding Star--
> Our Star of Destiny.[14]

---

[14]Ibid., p. 6.

Chapter IV

GARVEY'S THEOLOGICAL MOTIFS

Martin Luther, the prime mover of the Protestant Reformation, Menno Simons, the architect of the Mennonite Movement and John Wesley, the Father of Methodism, did not set out to systmatically outline a theology in their struggle to express deep religious concerns among their people. A systematic approach of their contribution to theology was put together by their understudies and disciples, and by theologians and students ofhistory, after the fact. Their theologies were reflective of the spiritual concerns which they expressed as they struggled personally with their faith, and as they looked at and evaluated the ecclesiastical structures, the theology, the ethics, and the socio-politics of their day. From their personal religious struggles and dialog with others, they espoused concepts of God, Christ, Spirit, Humanity, Salvation, the Kingdom of God, among other ideas. But it all began in a religious setting or as a response to a religious setting. Today, one can read books and dissertations on the theology of Martin Luther, Menno Simons and John Wesley.

Marcus Garvey did not set out to outline a theology, rather, he bagan with an ideology--an exegesis of Black existence, both in its chronological and cultural essence--and made it functional. However, he looked at his people, not in a particular geographical/cultural/religious/social location, but in a universal/cosmic/transnational sense, and he presented them with the good news--who their God was, and who Christ was, and therefore who they were and are. From this approach Garvey can be regarded as a functional theologian, in that he expressed deep religious concerns as he looked at his people in their historical setting, and raised questions in relationship to what was, what is, and what ought to be.

Unlike Martin Luther, Menno Simons and John Wesley, Marcus Garvey's theological reflection did not evolve out of an ecclesiastical or academic setting. Nor was Garvey particularly surrounded by noted scholars, theologians or students of history who afforded him constructive and critical dialog.

Garvey had a vision in which he perveived an
independent African nationality for the Black Race,
and declared that the time had come for the Black
Race to carve out a pathway for themselves in the
course of life. His main thrust was to demythologize
the Black Race's conception of God, Christ, Humanity
and Salvation and to redefine them in the light of
his concept of Ethiopianism--the future redemption
of Africa as a means of gaining full humanity.

Theology for Marcus Garvey was not only the
immediate occasion for the development of an
ecclesiastical institution such as the African
Orthodox Church, an arm of the UNIA, but it also
inspired the drive for a cosmic endeavor, a grand
design, a Christian Confraternity on a scale as
huge as human skill and effort could achieve.
Randall K. Burkett in his book Black Redemption--
Churchmen Speak for The Garvey Movement, said of
Garvey:

> "One illuminating way of viewing
> Marcus Garvey is to see him as a
> theologian concerned with constructing
> a coherent view of God, man, and the
> world, and of the meaning of the events
> which had shaped and were shaping the
> lives of Africans both at home and in
> the Diaspora . . . and the way in which
> he used religious language to express the
> goals of the UNIA.[1]

Garvey self-consciously endeavored to construct this
coherent view by which his followers could interpret
their historical experience as a people.

Therefore, the starting point for this approach
to the theology of Garvey is God, the Creator and
Sovereign Power of the Human Race. However, in order
to address the theocentric question, Garvey situated
himself chronologically and culturally in the course
of human history, and specifically the history of the
Black Race, and addressed God from the context of a
great civilization in human history. His theology

---

[1]Randall K. Burkett, Black Redemption:
Churchmen Speak for the Garvey Movement (Philadelphia,
1978), p. 24.

is bipolar—both anthropocentric and theocentric.

Garvey began his theology with an anthropology which affirmed the equality of the human race, then pointed to the historical experience of the Black Race as a mighty Race, self-affirming, and having an equal place in the course of human civilization; but this affirmation of the equality of the human race was based on the biblical doctrine of God the Creator and Sovereign Power of the entire human race. In this overarching view of humanity, Garvey presented a justification for the redemption of the Black Race in the present age. Garvey's aim was not to create a "world view" for the human race, but rather to address himself to the particular historical experience of the Black Race, and to raise the questions in relationship to what was, what is, and what ought to be. These questions also had to do with the fundamental contradiction the Black Race was experiencing between existence and essence.

Garvey's interest in the Black Race was not simply past-oriented but directed towards the future. His key intellectual concepts were "origin" and "goal". He viewed the Black Race in their present state as having their origin in God, and therefore potentially good or "mighty". With this perception of goodness as something pertaining to the divine, Garvey attempted to reconnect the fallen state of the Black Race in their present historical experience with that of the self-affirming state of the Black Race in their past historical experience, using the primitive African Society as the Exemplar, and Jesus the Resurrected One as Liberator, to offer a future promise of redemption.

A.   GOD

Garvey believed, as all Africans believed, in One Almighty God, the Creator of the Universe. However, there were numerous ways of expressing the one-god concept. God might be identified with the sun and called the Sun God, or, as a variation of this, He might be called the Sky God. The numerous other gods, far from being in conflict with the One Almighty God, were a necessary part of His divine plan--the earth, water, illness, health, fertility, planting, harvest, war, hunting, fishing, rain, etc. Each family or clan might or might not have its own clan god, and each member of the family might or might not have his own personal god. This belief that the spirit of the Creator or the Universal God permeates all of His creations is at the very heart of Garvey's concept of God.

For Garvey the objective essence of God was colorless in that He was conceived as a spirit, as was taught in the Universal Negro Catechism a book of religious knowledge for the Black Race:

Q.   What is God?
A.   God is a spirit, that is to say,
     He is without body, or visible form.

Q.   Are there more Gods than one?
A.   No, there is but One living and
     true God.

Q.   Mention some of the attributes of
     God.
A.   He is everlasting, omnipotent,
     omniscient, omnipresent, and of
     infinite wisdom, goodness, truth,
     love, holiness, justice and mercy.

Q.   By what title do we address God?
A.   "Our Father in Heaven".

Q.   Why is God called "Father"?
A.   Because He is the Creator of all
     beings, visible and invisible, and
     the Maker of all things in the
     natural world.

Q. Are all human beings then the
children of God?
A. Certainly, He is the great All-Father,
and all members of the human race
are His children.[2]

However, Garvey felt that the logic of an all Black
World demanded a Black God:

Q. What is the color of God?
A. A spirit has neither color, nor
other natural parts, nor qualities.

Q. But do we not speak of His hands,
His eyes, His arms, and other parts?
A. Yes; it is because we are able to
think and speak of Him only in human
and figurative terms.

Q. If, then, you had to think or speak
of the color of God, how would you
describe it?
A. As black, since we are created in
His image and likeness.

Q. On what would you base your assumption
that God is black?
A. On the same basis as that taken by
white people when they assume that
God is of their color.[3]

While Garvey was content to have his followers
remain within any (Black-led) religious organization,
whether Protestant or Catholic, Christian or non-
Christian, he was not willing for them to retain the
religious ideals and conceptualizations of another
race. He specifically and most emphatically rejected
the concept of God as white. As he declared on one
occasion:

If the white man has the idea of a

---

[2]Reverend George Alexander McGuire, comp.,
Universal Negro Catechism (Universal Negro Improvement
Association, 1921), p. 2.

[3]Ibid., p. 3.

white God, let him worship his God
as he desires . . . We, as Negroes,
have found a new ideal. Whilst
our God has no color, yet it is human
to see everything through one's own
spectacles, and since the white people
have seen their God through white
spectacles, we have only now started
out (late though it be) to see our
God through our own spectacles . . .
We Negroes believe in the God of
Ethiopia, the everlasting God--God
the Father, God the Son, and God
the Holy Ghost, the one God of all
ages. That is the God in Whom we
believe, but we shall worship Him
through the spectacles of Ethiopia.[4]

While Garvey conceived God as spirit, in terms of
the existential appropriation of God he argued that
God for Blacks must be conceived as "the God of
Ethiopia","the Black God".

Garvey turned to the scriptures for his
justification for the rejection of the White God.
He cited not only the Psalmist's prophecy concerning
Ethiopia:

Princes shall come out of Egypt;
Ethiopia shall soon stretch out her
hands unto God. (Psalm 68:31).

but also the Mosaic law against idolatry:

Thou shalt not make unto thee any
graven image, or any likeness of anything that is in heaven above, or that
is in the earth beneath, or that is in
the water under the earth: Thou shalt
not bow down thyself to them, nor serve
them: for I the Lord thy God am a
jealous God. (Exodus Ch. 20:4,5)

---

[4]Amy Jacques Garvey, ed., Philosophy and Opinions
of Marcus Garvey (New York, 1969), I, p. 44.

and declared that:

> Every man is a pattern of God . . . and
> all of God's creatures go to make God.
> All men being part of God, thus Black
> men must see that it is idolatrous to
> make God white. When you bow to a
> graven image, when you bow to the God
> of another species, you dishonor the
> God that is in you, and you . . . abase
> the God of your existence and commit a
> sin against the Holy Ghost . . . Therefore,
> the UNIA desires every Negro to destroy
> the image of the white God that you
> have been taught to bow to.[5]

Garvey did not see how Blacks could be true to the
cause of the redemption of Africa with a concept of
God that stemmed from the white community. He
contended that Blacks should conceptualize God
through the Black experience and Whites should view
God through their own experience. Garvey did not
argue that God literally became Black. But he
asserted that when Blacks view God, He takes on
the identity and particularity of the Black
experience.

Garvey had much more to say about God, however,
than that He must not be conceived by Black men as
white. Garvey did not conceive of God as apassive,
uninvolved reality. He viewed God as a God of both
war and peace:

> God is a bold Sovereign--A Warrior Lord.
> The God we worship and adore is a God
> of War as well as a God of Peace. He
> does not allow anything to interfere
> with His power and authority. The
> greatest battle ever fought was not
> between the Kaiser of Germany on the
> one hand and the Allied Powers on the
> other, it was between Almighty God on
> the one hand and Lucifer the Archangel on the

---

[5]Marcus Garvey's address "Africa and the Negro",
delivered at the Florida Avenue Presbyterian Church,
Washington, D.C., 16 January 1924. Negro World 15:25
(2 February 1924), p. 7.

other . . . the whole universe shook
as the battle raged between the two
opposing forces, and as God the Creator
gained the upper hand of Lucifer,
what did He do? Did He hoist the white
flag of peace? No, God Almighty, God
the Omnipotent took hold of Lucifer
and flung him from the heights of
Heaven to the depths of hell, thereby
proving that He is a God of War as well
as a God of Peace. And when anyone
trangresses His power He goes to war
in defence of His rights.[6]

In the confidential Lesson Guides written for his
school of African Philosophy, Garvey sought to
characterize otherattributes of God. For instance
Garvey declared that God must be understood as
Universal Intelligence:

There is a God and we believe in Him.
He is not a person nor a physical being.
He is a spirit and He is Universal
Intelligence. Never deny that there
is a God. God being Universal
Intelligence created the universe out
of that intelligence. It is
intelligence that creates. Man is a
part of the creation of Universal
Intelligence, and man was created in
the image and likeness of God only
by his intelligence. It is the
intelligence of man that is like God,
but man's intelligence is only a
unitary principle of God's Universal
Intelligence.[7]

Garvey asserted that God is also absolute power.
This is a power that man cannot deny:

There is a God.

---

[6]Garvey, Philosophy of Opinions, I, p. 43.

[7]Lesson 6, "God", Intelligence, Education,
Universal Knowledge and How to Get it. (Mimeographed,
n.d.), p. 1.

No man can say there is no God,
because no man is like God. Man is
limited in his intelligence at the
most and man knows how insufficient
he is between life and death--that
he is born without his knowledge and
dies without his will or wish; when
his birth and death must logically and
naturally be controlled by somebody
else.

It could not be man because man is
always man whether he be a big man or
small man. So power that gives birth
and causes death must be greater than
man's power. Whatsoever that power
is, it must be an absolute power.
Some men call it by different names
but all mean the same thing and it
is God.[8]

Garvey perceived power as sonething pertaining to
the divine.

Another attribute of God that Garvey lifted up
was that of God being on the side of the strong.
Garvey used this illustration to substantiate his
view:

I believe with Napoleon. When someone
asked him, "On what side is God?" he
replied, "God is on the side of the
strongest battalion". Napoleon was
right. He had a true concept of God.
God is really on the side of the
strongest people because God made all
men equal and He never gave superior
power to any one class or group of
people over another, and anyone who
can get the advantage over another
is pleasing God, because that is
the servant who has taken care of God's

---

[8]Lesson 14, "Self Initiative", ibid., pp. 2-3.

command in exercising authority over
the world.[9]

This was Garvey's attempt to help the Black race
realize their potential. Garvey informed them that
God was on the side of the powerful and the strong.
By this he meant that Blacks must become strong and
powerful as a race, and by so doing God would work
in their behalf. Garvey therefore issued a command
to the Black people--"Up You Mighty Race".

In pointing to another attribute of God, Garvey
used the oft-repeated phrase "God is no respecter
of persons", and declared that God had to be a God
of absolute impartiality and fairness:

> There can be no God if there be
> inequality in the creation or in the
> creative purpose of God. And there
> could be no God that would create a
> race to be a race of slaves and another
> to be one of masters. That race, this
> race of slaves, would reject such a God.

> There is no God who would create me a
> Black man, to be a hewer of wood and
> a drawer of water. It is a lie. It
> is a damned lie. If there is such a
> God, then I would have to look for
> another God. But there is no such God.
> The God that exists, the God that I
> love, the God that you also love and
> adore, is a God of Love, a God of
> Mercy, a God of Charity and a God
> that is no respecter of persons. Such
> a God I worship; Such a God I adore;
> and Such a God I know would never
> place me here especially to be a hewer
> of wood, a drawer of water, a picker of
> cotton and a laborer in a cane field.
> He placed me here As My Sovereign Lord
> to make of life whatsoever I desire
> to do. If I want to be an industrial
> captain, it is all left to my selection.
> God has no plantation; He is not an

---

[9]Garvey, Philosophy of Opinions, I, p. 44.

economist; He has nothing to do with
the affairs of men or the economic
arrangements of humanity. Otherwise
He would be an unfair God.[10]

On the basis of this premise of God's impartiality and fairness, Garvey found himself putting
forth two varying positions. On the one hand, he
argued that whereas God is not responsible for a
race's being in or out of slavery, the onus and the
fault had to borne by the enslaved race itself:

> Some of us flatter ourselves to
> believe that God is with us and God
> is being who is taking care of us in
> this serfdom and peonage and slavery that
> we are enduring. God is vexed with you
> because you are subordinating the
> powers that He gave to you.[11]

Garvey insisted that the Black Race does not have to
remain exploited, but must arise with the power that
is within to compel the respect of humankind. He
cited the rise of the British nation as an example:

> The great British nation was once a
> race of slaves. In their own country
> they were not respected because the
> Romans went there, brutalized and
> captured them, took them over to Rome
> and kept them in slavery. They were
> not respected in Rome because they
> were regarded as a slave race. But
> the Briton did not always remain a
> slave. As a freed man he went back
> to his country (Britain) and built up
> a civilization of his own, and by his
> self-reliance and initiative he forced
> the respect of mankind and maintains
> it until today.[12]

---

[10]Negro World 14:6 (24 March 1923), p. 7.

[11]Negro World 11:10 (22 October 1921), p.2.

[12]Garvey, Philosophy of Opinions, I, p. 16.

On another occasion Garvey argued:

> God is not going to save you. He has
> done all He possible could. He has
> given you a life to live, and if you
> do not exercise your own will in
> your own behalf you will be lost.
> God does not interfere with the
> temporal things of life; He does not
> interfere with the political destiny of
> races and nations; God is concerned with
> the spiritual destiny of man and not
> the political destiny of man.[13]

Garvey also took the position that the Black Race
must not rely on the White Race or put the blame of
their enslavement on the White Race or on God.
Therefore, on still another occasion he said:

> There are two understandings of God
> . . . the scientific and the
> sentimental. The Negro assumes the
> Sentimental idea, and therein he
> makes his big mistake. We must not
> blame God for our servile condition,
> because God gave us our physical
> self and made us lords of creation
> on an equality with all other
> men; nor must we blame the white
> man, who is similarly using the
> ability given to him by God. We
> have only ourselves to blame. "The
> fault is not in our stars, but in
> ourselves, that we are underlings."[14]

It was Garvey's argument that a scientific God had
empowered man with a will to act, and then threw
him back on his own resources either to survive or
to be destroyed.

On the other hand, although Garvey frequently
espoused the concept of an impartial God who had
created man with the potential to act on his own

---

[13]Negro World 13:15 (25 November 1922), p. 2.

[14]Negro World 12:4 (11 March 1922), p. 9.

behalf, and repeatedly insisted that Gar should
not be asked for the assistance that one should give
oneself, Garvey affirmed God's special action on
behalf of the Black Race:

> If humanity is regarded as made up of
> the children of God, and God loves all
> humanity--we all know that--then God
> will be more pleased with that race
> that protects all humanity than with
> that race that outrages all humanity.
> Up to now, we have found no race in
> power that has held out a helping hand
> and protection to all humanity, and it
> is apparent that that position is left
> for the new Ethiopia. Let us, therefore,
> continue our journey, man. I believe
> when we reach the goal we shall reign
> forever, because we shall be the elect
> of God. He must have had His purpose
> when he took us through the rigors of
> slavery for more than two hundred and
> fifty years . . . There must be some
> wonderful purpose of God in bringing
> us through all we had to endure in the
> past three hundred years, down to the
> present, and I attribute it to that
> prophecy of God that His children
> shall one day stretch forth their hands
> again unto Him.[15]

Garvey did not emphasize this theme of "chosenness"
as much as he spoke of an impartial God who had
created humanity with the capacity to act on their
own behalf. Therefore one must assume that Garvey
only drew upon the "chosenness" theme in connection
with the Psalmist's prophecy. To the extent that
Garvey on one occasion declared:

> Otherwise I would not believe in God;
> but I am persuaded to believe in Him
> because He Himself said, 'Princes shall
> come out of Egypt and Ethiopia shall
> stretch forth her hands unto God.[16]

---

[15]Negro World 11:22 (14 January 1922), p. 3.

[16]Negro World 13:15 (25 November 1922), p. 2.

This theme of God's special action on behalf of the Black Race was subordinate in Garvey's thinking to his view of the Black Race as having their origin in God and therefore potentially good and mighty. Garvey saw this potential for good as unlimited.

Garvey's theology of God is based on a firm doctrine of the goodness of creation and the accessibility of the commandments of divine goodness to the human situation. He saw human culture as a process within and part of a wider cosmic process. It was not simply the wistful projection of his own wishes and beliefs in what the Black Race can achieve, rather, Garvey affirmed the theology of God as Creator of all humanity, and saw the Black Race in their present state as having their origin in God, and therefore potentially good and mighty. Garvey's God is not the God who is the sole possession of the Black Race, but God of all Creation.

B. CHRIST

As Garvey did in his conception of God, he viewed
Jesus Christ first of all as the begotten Son of God
whose special mission was to take the form of man in
order to teach man how to lift himself back to God.
His concept of the Universal mission of Christ
extended to all humanity:

> Q. Who is Jesus Christ?
> A. The Redeemer of all mankind.[17]

Garvey even found it necessary to offer a defense of
the very idea of a Christ, declaring that:

> If Christ as man never existed, but
> was only an assumption it would have
> been a glorious assumption to set man
> a spiritual high example of how he
> should live.[18]

It is interesting to discover, however, that Garvey
was unsure of the historicity of Jesus and to claims
that He was the Christ. However, it is difficult to
ascertain whether Garvey's doubts about the
historicity of Jesus as Christ were a reaction
against the emphasis which White Christians placed
on the "Jesus, meek and mild", and the Jesus who
preached about "turning the other check", or whether
he simply could not accept as intellectually palatable
the Risen Christ of orthodox Christianity which the
then flourishing "Form criticism" was bring into
question.

It should be noted that this movement rose under
the leadership of such scholars as K.L. Schmidt
(Der Rahmen der Geschichte Jesu, 1919), Martin
Dibelius (Die Formgeschichte des Evangeliums, 1919),
Rudolf Bultmann (Jesus, 1925), and B.S. Easton (The
Gospel Before the Gospels, 1928, Christ in the
Gospels, 1930). However, the leading exponent of
"Form-criticism" in English was R.H. Lightfoot

---

[17]McGuire, Universal Negro Catechism, p. 3.

[18]Lesson 6, "Christ", Intelligence (Mimeographed,
1937), p. 1.

(History and Interpretation in the Gospels, 1935).
Some words of R.H. Lightfoot will be sufficient
reminder here of its main tenets, in Garvey's own
claim to the uncertainty of the historicity of Jesus.
In his Bampton Lectures (1934) Lightfoot said of the
Form critics:

> They remind us that the early Church is
> by no means likely to have expressed
> itself at once in a literary way, and
> they believe, first, that in the
> earliest years memories and traditions
> of the words and deeds of Jesus were
> only handed from mouth to mouth, and,
> secondly, that they were valued, not
> so much . . . in and for themselves,
> as for their importance in solving
> problems connected with the life and
> needs of the young churches. These
> needs, they think, would be chiefly
> concerned with mission preaching,
> catechetical teaching, demonstration
> of the content and meaning of the
> Christian life, refutation of Jewish
> and other objections,and, perhaps
> above all, worship.[19]

The net result, in the hands of many Form Critics,
was to regard the New Testament picture as affording
us very little knowledge of the historical Jesus.
The Gospels, in Lightfoot's well-known words, "yield
us little more than a whisper of his voice; we
trace in them but the outskirts of his ways."[20]

Despite Garvey's seeming uncertainty about the
historical Jesus as Christ, he adopted the stance
that one should not doubt the existence of Christ,
by way of the following illustration:

> There is no cause to doubt that Christ
> lived, not because you did not see Him

---

[19]R.H. Lightfoot, History and Interpretation in
The Gospels (London, 1935), pp. 30-31.

[20]Ibid., p. 225.

> yourself and feel Him yourself or
> touch Him yourself as Thomas did
> why should you doubt His existence,
> for it you can doubt that, you may
> as well doubt that your great
> grandfather ever lived, because you
> never saw him nor touched him, but
> logically there is fair assumption
> for you to believe that your grand-
> father whom you knew must have had
> a father, to be born must have had
> such a father, and he must have
> logically been your great grandfather.[21]

In any case he had no difficulty in accepting as the
highest ideal for all humanity both the central
teaching of Jesus, which was love, and Jesus as the
model of the moral life. Garvey indicated that the
New Testament revealed the life of Christ as an
exemplary one, and presented the teachings of Christ
as paramount for the Black Race:

> The greatest thing that Christ taught
> was love. Love thy neighbor as thy-
> self, do unto others as you would
> have them do to you. In these
> statements are wrapt up the highest
> idealism of a Godhead in the
> relationship of a father with his
> children. There has been no greater
> philosophy in the history of mankind.
> Support the philosophy and never
> change change until God manifest
> himself to the contrary, which is
> not likely.[22]

Just as was the case in his discussion of the nature
of God, Garvey insisted that Jesus Christ be conceived historically as a Black man. One of the most
spectacular of the elaborate ceremonials which took
place under UNIA auspices, and the event which
probably caused more comment throughout the United

---

[21]Burkett, Black Redemption, p. 36.

[22]Ibid., p. 37.

States, in both the white and black press, than any other in Liberty Hall, was the divine service at which occurred the canonization of the Lord Jesus Christ as the Black Man of Sorrows, and also the canonization of the Blessed Virgin Mary as a Black woman.

At that convention a resolution was passed to the effect "that though God is a spirit, as we all know, nevertheless when we visualize Him, He must be in our own image and likeness". Remarked an old woman from Alabama, "No white man would die on the cross for me". A delegate from Mississippi said, "The Man of Sorrows ain't nothing else but a Colored Man". Reverend J. Barbour of Abyssinia referred to John caught up in the grand Council of God on the Isle of Patmos, describing Christ as "a Black Man with feet that shone as polished brass, hair of lamb's wool, and eyes with flame of fire".[23] In addition to speeches on this subject, paintings of the Black Christ, "Man of Sorrows", and a Black Madonna and Babe, were paraded by robed choristers.

Implicit in Garvey's teaching on the doctrine of Christ is a principled universalism in Christ. For Garvey's claim was not that Jesus Christ was of pure African descent, but it was evident that Christ had in his veins the blood of all mankind, and belonged to no particular race. Garvey made this a part of his catechetical instructions:

> Q. Of what race was Jesus Christ?
> A. The Hebrew race, through
>   Abraham, Judah, David and others.
>
> Q. Of what larger group is the
>   Hebrew race a part?
> A. The Semitic.
>
> Q. Was there any admixture of other
>   blood than Semitic in the veins of
>   Jesus?
> A. Yes.

---

[23]Amy Jacques Garvey, Garvey and Garveyism (New York, 1970), pp. 140-141.

60

Q. Give an instance.
A. Pharez, the Son of Judah, and
   an ancestor of Jesus, was born
   of Tamar, a woman of Canaan and
   a descendant of Ham.

Q. Mention another instance.
A. Rahab, the mother of Boaz,
   who was the great-grandfather of
   David was also a Canaanite woman.[24]

On another occasion in the "School of African
Philosophy", Garvey discussed the doctrine of Christ
in one of his lessons, indicating that:

> In reading Christian Literature and
> accepting the doctrine of Jesus Christ
> lay special claim to your association
> with Hesus and the Son of God. Show
> that whilst the white and yellow worlds,
> that is to say--the worlds of Europe
> and Asia Minor persecuted and crucified
> Jesus the Son of God, it was the Black
> Race through Simon the Black Cyrenian
> who befriended the Son of God and took
> up the Cross and bore it alongside of
> Him to the heights of Calvary. The
> Roman Catholics, therefore, have no
> rightful claim to the Cross nor is any
> other professing Christian before the
> Negro. The Cross is the property of the
> Negro in his religion because it was
> he who bore it.

> Never admit that Hesus Christ was a
> white man, otherwise he would not be
> the Son of God and God to redeem all
> mankind. Jeius Christ had the blood
> of all races in his veins, and tracing
> the Jewish race back to Abraham and to
> Moses, from which Jesus sprang through
> the line of Jesse, you will find Negro
> blood everywhere, so Jesus had much of
> Negro blood in Him.[25]

---

[24]McQuire, Universal Negro Catechism, p. 5.

[25]Lesson 1, Intelligence, p. 11.

61

The over-all impact of Garvey's remarks on the
significance of the presence of Negro blood in
Jesus' veins was to reinforce a particular
interpretation of Christ's role in the history of the
Black race. This was accomplished primarily through
emphasis on the centrality of Simon the Cyrenian,
the Black man who had been forced to bear Jesus'
Cross up Calvary Hill. By virtue of this unique deed
it was argued that the Black race stood in a special
relationship to Jesus; and on occasion this special
act of Simon's was publicly contrasted with the act
of betrayal by the white man who, it was suggested,
had to bear responsibility for Christ's crucifixion.
In a speech portraying Jesus as a model for the
present world, and as one who bore undeserved suffering, and who thereby has a special affection for
those who are despised, rejected, and forced to
bear unmerited suffering, Garvey declared:

> Give us the standard bearer of Christ;
> let Him lead and we shall follow, Christ
> the crucified, Christ the despised,
> we appeal to you for help, for succor
> and for leadership . . . Oh Jesus
> the Christ, oh Jesus the Redeemer,
> when white men pierced your side out
> of which blood and water gushed forth,
> it was a Black man in the person of
> Simon the Cyrenian who took the Cross
> and bore it on heights of Calvary. As
> he bore it in the past to lighten
> your burden as you climbed your Calvary,
> so now, when we are climbing our
> Calvary and the burden being heavy--
> Jesus we ask You to help us on the
> journey up the heights.[26]

This model of Jesus as Suffering Servant was always
balanced, however, with the model of Jesus as The
Great Reformer:

> If we could see the sufferings of
> Christ, if we could see the very
> crucifixion of Christ, then we
> would see the creature, the being
> spiritual that God would have us to

26Negro World 11:2 (27 August 1921), p. 3.

be; and knowing ourselves as
we do, we could well realize how
far we are from God . . . the world
derided Him; the world scoffed at
Him; they called Him all kinds of
names. He was an imposter; He was a
disturber of the public peace; He was
not fit to be among good society; He
was an outcast; He was a traitor to
the Kings . . .

Christ was the first great reformer . . .
There is one lesson we can learn from
the teachings of Christ . . . The
spiritual doctrines of Jesus were
righteous; The doctrines of Jesus
were just, and even though He died
nearly nineteen hundred years ago,
what has happened? After the lapse
of nineteen hundred years His religion
is the greates moving force in the
world today, morally and spiritually.
It shows you, therefore, the power of
a righteous cause.[27]

It must be noted that Garvey chose his own
categories to appropriate the meaning of Jesus Christ
for the Black race in their existential situation.
Unlike the theologian Oscar Cullman, in referring to
the titles of Jesus, who declared:

The New Testament neither is able nor
intends to give information about how
we are to conceive the being of God
beyond the history of revelation,
about whether it really is a being
only in the philosophical sense. It
intends rather to report the great
event of God's revelation in Christ . . .
Even today there is no other method
of Christological perception besides
the one given in John 5-8 . . . These
are the sources of early Christian

27Garvey's Christmas Eve sermon entitled "Christ
the Greatest Reformer", Philosophy of Opinions, II,
pp. 28-30.

Christological conviction. For
the modern man there are no others.[28]

Garvey characterized Jesus in terms of the needs and
existential experience which the Black race was
encountering, and thereby developed categories that
he deemed relevant for his people. He saw Jesus as
a Great Reformer, one who was rough, unyielding,
uncompromising, fearing only God:

> All true warriors know no fear. Our
> friends are fainthearted, but Jesus
> Christ was the greatest radical the
> world ever saw. Jesus opposed wrong.
> His program was to lift up humanity
> and save mankind.[29]

This model of Jesus as the Great Reformer provided
Garvey with the necessary impetus to challenge the
Black race and broad and liberal-minded white men
to work for black reform, and for justice's sake
to give unto each and everyone his due. In a speech
on "Racial Reforms and Reformers" Garvey cited the
reformer in human civilization as the key person to
lift the backward and non-progressive to the common
standard of progress and civilization:

> In this conflict of life each human
> being finds a calling. Some of us are
> called to be preachers, ministers of the
> Gospel, politicians, statesmen,
> industrialists, teachers, philosophers,
> laborers, and reformers. To the reformer,
> above all, falls the duty or obligation
> of improving human society, not to the
> good of the selfish few, but to the
> benefit of the greatest number. The
> history of the world and of the human
> race tells us the story of the reformer,

---

[28]Oscar Cullman, The Christology of The New
Testament (Philadelphia, 1959), pp. 327-328.

[29]Negro World 11:25 (4 February 1922), p. 9.

64

of his trials, persecution and
suffering in his efforts to reach
the heart of man, in creating there
a common sympathy for his brother.
If it was not a Christ, it was a St.
Augustine, a Luther or a Caesar,
Alfred the Great, Garibaldi, Lincoln
or a McSwiney. But all down the
line of human progress we have met
the man ready to suffer and to die
to make others free while a light-
hearter selfish populace laughs at
him and passes by the effort.[30]

Garvey viewed the role of leadership as a call of
service to all of humanity, and contended that it
was the duty and obligation of men not to only act
human, but to act as Christ in dispensing justice,
love and mercy to all. His theology of Christ
revealed Garvey's sensitivity towards the need of
the human race as a whole working together in love
without endangering the rights of either. Garvey
presented Christ as the Great Reformer who taught
humanity the way, and who served as a model for other
great reformers in the common cause of justice,
liberty, freedom and true human independence, knowing
thereby no color or no race:

> The example set by our Lord and Master
> nineteen hundred years ago is but the
> example that every reformer must make
> up his mind to follow if we are indeed
> to serve those to whom we minister.[31]

Garvey further asserted that such service can be
rendered by persons of all races on behalf of Black
humanity. In a speech on "Black Reform" Garvey cited
the following example:

> There is a fraternity of humanitarians,
> unknown through it be, that is working
> for a true solution of our human problems.

---

[30]Garvey, _Philosophy of Opinions_, I, p. 7.

[31]_Ibid._, p. 88.

Wilberfore, Clarkston, Buxton, Lovejoy,
John Brown, white though they were,
had the vision of the future of men.
They worked for the freedom of Black
humanity; Therefore in the midst of
our Sorrow and the racial thought of
revenge come up the spirits of such
great humanitarians that silence
the tongue of evil; as in the White
race, so smong the Blacks, our beautiful spirits stand out, for wasn't
there a Douglass, a Washington and
even the typical Uncle Tom? We
hope that the humanitarians of today
of all races will continue to work in
furtherance of that ideal.[32]

Garvey pointed out that the essential principle of
true religion which Jesus taught is the universal
brotherhood of man growing out of the universal
Fatherhood of God, and therefore Christ did not go
exclusively to the classes but devoted His life to
all. In terms of Garvey's use of Jesus as a model,
this principle of true religion was to be exercised
by all persons, and especially the strong:

We need a better understanding of self,
as individuals, and may I not appeal to
the strong and mighty races and nations
of the world for a better and a closer
consideration and understanding of the
teachings of the man Christ, who went
about this world in His effort to
redeem fallen man? May I not say to
the strong, may I not say to the
powerful, that until you change your
ways there will be no salvation,
there will be no redemption, there will
be no seeing God face to face? God is
just, God is love, God is no respecter
of persons; God does not uphold
advantage and abuse to His own people;
God created mankind to the same rights
and privileges and the same opportunities,
and before man can see his God, man will
have to measure up in that love, in that

---

[32]Ibid., p. 10.

brotherhood that He desired us to
realize and know as taught to us by
His Son Jesus Christ.

Let us realize that we are our brother's
keeper; let us realize that we are of
one blood, created of one nation to
worship God the Common Father.[33]

Garvey warned his hearers that to follow Christ's
example would lead to resistance, which he argued
that all reformers and reform movements are subjected when they cease to preach a strictly spiritual
message and demand that existing social and economic
relationships be transformed. He characterized
Jesus as preaching a message that was both spiritual
and temporal. It was such a message, Garvey argued,
that brought about Jesus' crucifixion:

When Jesus came the privileged few
were taking advantage of the unfortunate
masses. Because the teaching of Jesus
sought to equalize the spiritual and
even the temporal rights of man, those
who held authority, sway and dominion
sought His liberty by prosecution,
sought His life by death. He was
called to yield up that life for the
cause He loved--because He was indeed
a great reformer.[34]

Garvey portrayed Christ as the Greatest Reformer the
world ever saw, one whose teachings was of a spiritual
and moral nature. He characterized the teachings of
Jesus as a force in the cause of justice, freedom,
and righteousness in the world. Although Garvey
realized that human beings had not changed much, in
that they would crucify Christ if He were to return
to the world today, born in the same lowly state,
born of the same humble parentage, and attempted to
preach the same redemption, he affirmed the teachings
of Christ by declaring:

---

[33]Ibid., p. 31.

[34]Ibid., pp. 87-88.

But there is one lesson we can learn
from the teachings of Christ. Even
though man in the ages may be hard
in heart and hard in soul, that
which is righteous, that which is
spiritually just, even though the
physical man dies, the righteous
cause is bound to live . . .

Jesus the man was not respected,
Jesus the man was not adored, Jesus
the man was not even loved by His own
people, and for that they crucified
Him; but the spiritual doctrines of
Jesus were righteous; the doctrines of
Jesus were just, and even though He
died nearly nineteen hundred years
ago, what has happened? After the
lapse of nineteen hundred years His
religion is the greatest moving force
in the world today, morally and
spiritually. It shows you, therefore,
the power of a righteous cause.[35]

Garvey claimed that Jesus who was the first Great
Reformer taught us the way; after Him followed the
other great reformers who shared the same fate.
But, declared Garvey, "the doctrine, the teachings
of Jesus, will rise again on the wings of time and
flourish as the green bay tree."[36]

---

[35]Ibid., p. 30.

[36]Ibid., p. 33.

C. MAN

> In the beginning God created man in
> His own image and likeness and gave
> him dominion over the birds of the
> air and the fish in the sea (Genesis
> Ch. 1:26)

Herein lies for Garvey the Basic concept of who God
is. He is the God of Creation whose authority rests
in creating and empowering man with attributes of
his Maker. This biblical concept of God underlies
Garvey's theology of man, in which he attributed to
man an inherent creative power to rule and govern
his environment, and thereby issued this challenge:

> The cry of the Universal Negro Improvement
> Association is for real men--men of
> character, men of courage, men of
> confidence, men of faith, men who
> believe that all creation is but
> the domain of man and that above
> man there is no authority but God.
> When the Creator created His master-
> piece, Man, and placed him in the
> world as lord of His creation it
> was meant that man should establish
> sovereignty over the world--that he
> should subdue all things and use
> them to his own satisfaction and
> shape them to his own will. God
> never intended that man should
> expect Him to do for him that which
> he should do for himself.[37]

Garvey argued that the function of man is to harness
the elements, subdue and use them. In man lies the
power of mastery over all created things, and all
nature are at his command:

> Edison harnessed electricity. Today
> the world reflects the brilliancy of
> his grand illumination. Stephenson,

---

[37]Burkett, Black Redemption, p. 31.

through experiments, has given us
the use of the steam engine, and
today the railroad train flies
across the country at a speed of
sixty miles an hour. Marconi
conquered the currents of the air
and today we have wireless telegraphy
that flashes news across the continents
with a rapidity never yet known to
man. All this reveals to us that man
is the supreme lord of creation, that
in man lies the power of mastery, a
mastery of self, a mastery of all
things created, bowing only to the
Almighty Architect in those things
that are spiritual, in those things
that are divine.[38]

However, Garvey insisted that such power did not
extend over other human beings. Such power enriches
human life and fulfills the purposeof God for man.
For Garvey, God did not create any man or race without a goal or purpose in mind. He created every
man with possibilities for achievement, and for man
to think that he was created only to be what he is
and not what he has the possibilities of becoming
is to misunderstand God's reason for making man.
Why did God creat the Black man? Did he create him
to be a slave? Garvey answered in the following
manner:

> The man or woman who has no confidence
> in self is an unfortunate being, and is
> really a misfit in creation.
>
> God Almighty created each and everyone
> of us for a place in the world, and for
> the least of us to think that we were
> created only to be what we are and
> not what we can make ourselves, is to
> impute an improper motive to the
> Creator for creating us. God Almighty
> created us all to be free. That the
> Negro race became a race of slaves
> was not the fault of God Almighty, the
> Divine Master, it was the fault of the race.

---

[38]Garvey, Philosophy of Opinions, I, p. 28.

Sloth, neglect, indifference caused us
to be slaves. Confidence, conviction,
action will cause us to be free men
today.[39]

In this sense Garvey argued that men are arbiters of
their own destiny, and challenged the Black race to
a self-examination. He contended that their
allegiance should be to self first as men. For all
authority that meant the regulation of human affairs,
human society and human happiness was arrogated to
man by the Creator. The Black race, therefore had
a special responsibility to God, family, race and
country:

> Let no voice but your own speak to you
> from the depths. Let no influences but
> your own rouse you in time of peace
> and time of war; hear all, but attend
> only to that which concerns you. Your
> allegiance shall be to Your God, then
> to your family, race and country.
> Remember always that the Jew in his
> political and economic urge is always
> first a Jew; the White man is first
> a White man under all circumstances,
> and you can do no less than being
> first and always a Negro, and then
> all else will take care of itself.
> Let no one innoculate you with evil
> doctrines to suit their own conveniences.
> There is no humanity before that which
> starts with yourself. "Charity begins
> at home". First, to thyself be true,
> and thou canst not then be false to
> any man.[40]

Garvey would argue that, when men failed to recognize
that within them there is an inherent power that is
a part of God's creative process, their self-image

---

[39]Ibid., p. 37.

[40]John Heurik Clarke, ed., Marcus Garvey and
the Vision of Africa (New York, 1974), p. 158.

71

is weakened and they become helpless before other men. However, Garvey regarded this weakness as an affront to God, rather than the imposed will and dominance of others, and warned against this fatalist position:

> Some of us seem to accept the fatalist position, the fatalist attitude,that God accorded to us a certain position and condition, and therefore there is no need trying to be otherwise. The moment you accept such an opinion, the moment you harbor such an idea, you hurl an insult at the great God who created you, because you question Him for His love, you question Him for His mercy. God has created man, and has placed him in this world as the lord of the creation, as the sovereign of everything that you see, let it be land, let it be sea, let it be the lakes, rivers and everything therein. All that you see in creation, all that you see in the world was created by God for the use of man, and you four hundred million black souls have as much right to your possession in this world as any other race . . .

> I repeat that God created you masters of your own destiny, masters of your own fate, and you can pay no higher tribute to your Divine Master than function as man, as He created you.[41]

For Garvey it was more a question of differences between strong and weak races, but only in the sense that the Black race had failed to realize, to recognize, and to know themselves as other men have known and felt that there is nothing in the world that is above them except the influence of God. In an address on the subject of the differences between strong and weak races, Garvey said:

---

[41]Garvey, Philosophy of Opinions, I, pp. 90-91.

The difference between the strong
and weak races is that the strong
races seem to know themselves;
seem to discover themselves; seem
to realize and know fully that
there is but a link between them
and the Creator; that above them
there is no other but God and anything that bears human form is but
their equal in standing and to that
form there should be no obeisance;
there should be no regard for
superiority. Because of that
feeling they have been able to hold
their own in this world; they have
been able to take care of the
situation as it confronts them in
nature; but because of our lack of
faith and confidence in ourselves
we have caused others created in
a like image to ourselves, to take
advantage of us for hundreds of
years.[42]

Garvey appealed to the 400,000,000 Blacks to endeavor
to gain the same understanding that others have
gotten out of life, to think of nature as their
servant, and man as their partner through life. He
called for a new inspiration among the race that
they may go through the length and breadth of this
world achieving and doing as other men, as other
nations, and other races. Garvey constantly deplored
the feelings of inferiority which the Black race
displayed, and through his catechetical approach he
informed the race of their true heritage:

Q. How did God create man?
A. Male and female created He them
    after His own image, in knowledge,
    righteousness, and holiness, with
    dominion over all the earth and
    the lower animals.

---

[42]Ibid., pp. 91-92.

Q. Did God make any group or race
of men superior to another?
A. No; He created all races equal,
and of one blood, to dwell on all
the face of the earth.

Q. Is it true that the Ethiopian or
Black group of the human family
is the lowest group of all?
A. It is a base falsehood which is
taught in books written by white
men. All races were created
equal.

Q. What, then, is the chief reason
for the differences observed
among the various groups of
men?
A. Environment; that is conditions
connected with climate, opportunity,
necessity, and association with
others.[43]

On this same theme, Garvey declared in an editorial
entitled, "Man--As We Know Him":

And what is the difference between man--
the one who that towers as a giant above
the other who, like a pigmy, wallows
in the gutter? Because the giant man,
after discovering himself, utilizes
every ounce of his vitality and every
particle of his entire being to reach
out to the higher things that are within the reach of man. That is to say,
he hangs his hopes, he pins his confidence as high as human limitations,
that limitation that has been set only
by God Himself; in the exercise of his
will, that inner set character that
goes out to achieve, to conquer, to
subdue all things that are possible
to man. The other fellow--characterless
because of himself, inconfident because
of himself, hopeless because of himself--

---

[43]McGuire, Universal Negro Catechism, pp. 2-3.

> determines that it cannot be done,
> therefore will not try. No will, no
> mental force, no spiritual power,
> even though he was created with all
> these things, will he exert . . .
> When man reduces himself to become
> the slave and lackey of his fellow, he
> drags down the Spiritual Omnipotence of
> God in him, and God says "There shall
> be no other gods but Me."[44]

Garvey challenged the Black race to realize that
God created them to be real men, not pigmies, and
that God never created a superior man but them. He
argued that when they accepted a superior human
being to themselves, they admitted that there is a
superior God to the one who creates, and therefore
accepted an insult to the God that is within them.
He appealed to the Black race that if they would
understand themselves the more as others seemed to
do, they would in a short time find themselves
living in a new world surrounded with new conditions
and enjoying new pleasures. He regarded this
aspiration as a goal that was attainable in the 135
immediate future, and within the grasp of the Black
race:

> If four hundred million Negroes can
> only get to know themselves, to know
> that in them is a sovereign power,
> is an authority that is absolute,
> then in the next twenty-four hours
> we would have a great empire resur-
> rected not from the will of others
> to see us rise, but from our own
> determination to rise irrespective
> of what the world thinks.[45]

It was Garvey's view that God is only pleased with
man when he measures up to the higher spirituality
that is in him, which is no other than God Himself.

---

[44]Burket, Black Redemption, pp. 33-34.

[45]Ibid., p. 34.

To be a man in Garvey's eyes meant never to give up, never to depend upon others to do what one ought to do for oneself, and to be one who will not blame God, nature, or fate for one's condition. The difference between the strong and weak man, said Garvey was that the strong man went out and made conditions to suit himself. This applied both to individual men and to races.

The most definitive public statement of Garvey's theology of man was published in a front page editorial of the Negro World, and was entitled "Dissertation on Man". In this passage one can discern several key elements in his conception of the nature of man (some have been mentioned before), but in addition to emphasizing the structural change that has taken place in man since creation, Garvey stressed the need for a certain type of man, a real man, to make good in God's creation:

> Man is the individual who is able to shape his own character, master his own will, direct his own life, and shape his own ends.

> When God breathed into the nostrils of man the breath of life, made him a living soul, and bestowed upon him the authority of lord of creation, He never intended that that individual should descend to the level of a peon, a serf, or a slave, but that he should be always man in the fmllest possession of his senses, and with the truest knowledge of himself.

> But how changed has man become since creation? We find him today divided into different classes--the helpless imbecile class, the sycophantic class, the slave class, the servant class and the master class. These different classes God never created. He created man. But this individual has so retrograded, as to make it impossible to find him. It is so difficult to find a real man.

> As far as our race goes, I hardly believe that we can find one hundred

real men who are able to measure
up to the higher purpose of the
creation. It is because of this
lack of manhood in us as a race why
we have stagnated for several
centuries and now find ourselves at the
foot of the great human ladder.[46]

It was Garvey's view that there was a certain type of
man, the real man that would be able to make good in
God's creation. He difined that certain type as
men who build nations, governments and empires,
great monuments of commerce, industry and education.
These men realized the power given them by their
Creator God, exerted every bit of it to their own
good and to their posterity's. While, on the other
hand, four hundred million Blacks who claimed the
common Fatherhood of God and the Brotherhood of man,
have fallen back so completely, as to make themselves
the slaves and serfs of those who fully know themselves and have taken control of the world, which
was given to all in common to the Creator. Garvey
questioned the availability of real men in the Black
race:

> For the last four hundred years the
> Negro has been in the position of
> being commanded even as the lower
> animals are controlled. On race
> has been without a will; without
> a purpose of its own, for all this
> length of time. Because of that
> we have developed few men who are
> able to understand the strenuousness
> of the age in which we live.
>
> Where can we find in this race of
> ours real men. Men of character,
> men of purpose, men of confidence,
> men of faith who really know them-
> selves? I have come across so
> many weaklings who profess to be
> leaders, and in the test I have
> found them but slaves of a nobler

---

[46]*Negro World* 12:11 (29 April 1922), p. 1.

class. They perform the will of
their masters without question.[47]

Garvey characterized the real man as the man who will
never say die; the man who will never give up; the
man who will never depend upon others to do for him
what he ought to do for himself; the man who will
not blame God, who will not blame Nature, who will
not blame Fate for his condition; but the man who
will go out and make conditions to suit himself.
Garvey was disgusted with his own race, and was not
afraid to voice his disappointment as well as to
accept responsibility for creating a new environment
and mind set among Black people. In discussing the
lack of co-operation in the Black race, Garvey
declared:

> It is so hard, so difficult to find
> men who will stick to a purpose, who
> will maintain a principle, for the
> good of that purpose, and if there
> is a race that needs such men in
> the world today, God Almighty knows
> it is the race of which I am a member.

> The race needs men of vision and
> ability. Men of character and
> above all men of honesty, and that
> is so hard to find.

> But notwithstanding the lack of
> sympathetic co-operation, I have one
> consolation--that I cannot get away
> from the race, and so long as I am
> in the race and since I have sense and
> judgment enough to know what effects
> the race affects me, it is my duty to
> help the race to clear itself of those
> things that affect us in common.[48]

Garvey was much of a race patriot to identify with

---

[47]Garvey, Philosophy of Opinions, I, p. 38.

[48]Ibid., p. 49.

his people's hurt and oppression, and to seek to alleviate them in their condition.

Garvey's concept of the real man included men of other races whom Garvey admired. Though he was interested in men of his race whom he could count upon as being able to withstand the test of the leaders of the other races of the world. Garvey gave honor to those men who rendered unselfish service to others:

> Among the men in the world that I admire are such noble characters as David Lloyd George and Arthru J. Balfour of England; Clemencean, Briand and Poincare of France; Ishi and Katon of Japan; Lenin and Trotsky Russia; Gandhi of India; Griffith, Collins and De Valera of Ireland; Hughes, Harding and Wilson of America. In vain do I look for such characters in the Negro Race.[49]

Garvey affirmed the spiritual nature of this real man that he advocated. He regarded life not only in the physical sense but was always conscious of a higher life. It was to this higher spiritual life that Garvey challenged the Black race, assuring them that the day of triumph and authority to mete our justice will come and Africa may yet teach the higher principles of justice, love, mercy, and true brotherhood. In so doing, Garvey claimed that they will have removed themselves from the curse of a heartless, sinful, unjust world to a new temporal sphere, where man will live in peace and die in the consciousness of a new resurrection.

Garvey argued that Christ came to restore man to his spiritual kinship with his God, and therefore urged men of all races to practice a spirit of love, a spirit of charity, a spirit of mercy toward mankind; because in so doing they would bring God's kingdom down to earth. Man must not fail to understand his dual personality, as Garvey would argue. Man must live that true life, that perfect life as

---

[49]Burket, Black Redemption, p. 35.

spiritual beings, not forgetting that they are
physical also.

But Garvey contended that neither God nor Christ
is interested in the physical activities of man.
In that regard Christ cared so little for the physical that He offered Himself up and was satisfied
to go on the cross and let the physical die. God the
Father is interested in the spiritual of man, but
man's physical body is for his own protection.
Garvey urged the Black race to make their
interpretation of Christianity scientific--what it
ought to be, and blame not God, blame not the white
man for physical conditions for which they themselves
are responsible. Garvey provided this interpretation
in his attempt to offer a better understand to those
who were blaming God and Christ for their physical
ills:

> Some of us seem to believe that
> Christ and God the Father are
> responsible for all our ills--
> physical ills. They have nothing
> to do with our physical ills. I
> repeat, God is not and Jesus is not
> interested in the bodies of men.
> If you want to care for your body,
> that is the privilege and pre-
> rogative given to you by God.
> If you want to destroy it, that is
> the same privilege and prerogative
> He has given. If you want to commit
> suicide, that is your business.
> If you want to live, that is your
> business. God has given you the
> power; He has made you a free
> agent as far as the physical in life
> goes. All that God is interested in
> is the spiritual; That you cannot
> kill, because the moment you destroy
> the physical body God lays claim to
> the spiritual with which you are
> endowed. The spiritual is never
> yours. The spiritual is always
> God's but the physical is your own
> property. If you want to break your
> physical life up, that is all your
> business. God does not interfere and
> that should be the Negro's
> interpretation in this twentieth

century of Christ's religion.[50]

Garvey would argue that if one man enjoys life and another does not, God has absolutely nothing to do with the difference between the two individuals. It is purely a physical regulation left to man himself.

While man has the capacity, then, as a free agent, inasmuch as he is created in the image of an impartial God, the cruel and harsh fact is that for the most part he does not so behave. The dark side of man's nature, his capacity for evil, was by no means neglected in Garvey's theology of man. This theme is elaborated in the eleventh of his Lesson Guides written for the School of African Philosophy, in the chapter entitled "Man".

> Man because of his sin which caused him to have fallen from his high estate of spiritual cleanliness to the level of a creature, who acts only for his own satisfaction by the gift of freewill, must be regarded as a dangerous creature of life. When he wants he can be good, otherwise he is generally bad. If dealing with him you must calculate for his vices and his damnable evils. He is apt to disappoint you at any time therefore you cannot wholly rely on him as an individual. Always try to touch him with the hope of bringing out that which is good, but be ever on your guard to experience the worst that is in him, because he is always in conflict with himself as between good and evil.
>
> When he can profit from evil he will do it and forget goodness. This has been his behavior ever since his first record of his existence and his first contact with his fellows.

---

[50]Garvey, Phyilosophy of Opinions, I, pp. 32-33.

Can slew Abel for his success.
Jacob robbed Esan of his birthright and
down the ages of human history man
has been robbing, exploiting and
murdering man for gain.

The passion of man is in evidence
everywhere. It revolts against
affection, kindness and even love
when it has a personal object to
attain. Seek first to know him
then before you completely trust
him, because you are apt to be dis-
appointed. A man shakes your hand
today and tomorrow he is chief
witness against you for execution.
What is it that has caused him to
do that? It is his vileness. Know
it then that he is vile, and only
when you know him sufficiently may
you trust him as far as your
judgment would dictate.

It is generally evil, which gives
you evidence sufficient that man is
vile and only in remote instances
good. If you know it then, why take
the chance of always believing before
seeing? The taste of the pudding is
the proof of it. Know your man before
you believe. Never believe before
you know. Let your mission be always
to make man good, therefore talk to
man always from the loftiest pinnacle.
You may convert somebody, you may turn
a vile man good, and if you succeed in
doing this in even one instance you
have accomplished a great work.[51]

Garvey here illustrated man's capacity for evil, but
also spoke at least of the possibility of converting
him, of turning him from his evil ways and toward
good. The same covetousness of another's property
which drove Cain to slay his brother, Garvey
contended, has driven nation to rob from nation.

_____

[51]Lesson 11, "Man", Intelligence, pp. 1-3.

Therefore, Garvey asserted that the only appropriate category that men in groups can address other men in groups is power:

> Man is wicked, man is envious, man is rebellious, man is murderous, and you can expect very little of man. The only protection against injustice in man is power, financial power, educational power, scientific power, power of every kind; it is that power that the Universal Negro Improvement Association is encouraging Negroes to get for themselves.[52]

It was Garvey's view that power is the only argument that satisfies man. Except the individual, the race or the nation has power that is exclusive, argued Garvey, it meant that that individual, race or nation will be bound by the will of the other who possesses this great qualification. However, Garvey had a great vision for the Black race and inspired them with hope for the future and reminded them always that God created them lords of this creation. In prophetic and colorful language Garvey exclaimed:

> I have a vision of the future, and I see before me a picture of a redeemed Africa, with her dotted cities, with her beautiful civilization, with her million of happy children, going to and fro. Why should I lose hope, why should I give up and take a back place in this age of progress? Remember that you are men, that God created you Lords of this creation. Lift up yourselves, men, take yourselves out of the mire and hitch your hopes to the stars; yes, rise as high as the very stars themselves. Let no man pull you down, let no man destroy your ambition, because man is but your companion, your equal; man's your brother; he is not your lord; he is

---

[52]Negro World 12:25 (5 August 1922), pp. 3-4.

83

not your sovereign master.[53]

Garvey had an abiding confidence, a hope and a faith in the Black race and in God. A faith that he believed will ultimately take the Black race to that ancient place, that ancient position that the race once occupied, when Ethiopia was in her glory. Therefore, he believed that the Psalmist had great hopes of the Black race when he prophesied "Princes shall come out of Egypt and Ethiopia shall stretch forth her hands unto God".

Garvey's concept of man, his theology of man reached its high point in his graphic illustration of the immortality of man both body and spirit, and his challenge to man to never be afraid to die (change):

> Man never dies. Nothing dies. Man is made of body and spirit. The spirit is God. It is intelligence. The body of man is matter. It changes from living matter in the man to other matter in the soil. It is always the same matter. It doesn't die in the sense of how we understand death. It changes. When man sleeps and passes away in the flesh, he goes to earth that lives on, out of which other men and things are formed. All matter is related as man is related and the earth related to man. We eat ourselves over and over again. When we eat the apples, the banana, the fig, the cherry and the grape, when we drink the water, we are eating and drinking ourselves over and over again, so nothing is lost and nothing dies. So, do not be afraid of death because what you call death is only change and you are still in the universe, either in the Spirit of God to whom your spirit goes after the change or as matter which goes on forever.[54]

---

[53]Garvey, Philosophy of Opinions, I, p. 78.

[54]The New Negro World 1:11 (July 1942), p. 6.

Garvey would contend that all this reveals to us that man is the supreme lord of creation, that in man lies the power of mastery, a mastery of self, a mastery of all things created, bowing only to the Almighty Architect in those things that are spiritual, in those things that are divine. It was Garvey's desire to impress upon the four hundred million members of his race that their failings in the past, present and of the future would be through their failures to know themselves and to realize the true functions of man on this mundane sphere.

D. SALVATION/REDEMPTION

Garvey's concept of the dual nature of man--his
capacity for evil on the one hand and his potential
for creative power on the other hand--formed the basis
of his doctrine of salvation and redemption. It was
Garvey's persistent argument that salvation had to
lie within man's own grasp, in this case within the
grasp of the Black race, and not rest solely on other
races. Salvation would be achieved not by faith
alone, but by the persistent work of every man.

Garvey's concept of salvation/redemption was
rooted in the dual emphasis of work, self-reliance,
and his admonition to secure power by becoming aware
of the power within. Garvey viewed Jesus as the
Greatest Reformer who served as a model to empower
man to act for his own and his people's slavation.
Jesus was not Himself the instrument or vehicle of
salvation. Garvey argued that the example set by
Jesus nineteen hundred years ago was the example that
every reformer must make up his mind to follow if
they would serve humanity. The life of Jesus was
intended, according to Garvey, to show man that he
could lift himself to the highest plane of spirit
and human life. The mission of Jesus was to empower
man; His example was the power of a righteous cause.

The demand for power was argued most persuasively
in one of Garvey's Negro World editorials:

> Gradually, even though slowly, we
> getting to realize that the fight is
> now or never. We have to fight for a
> place in the world if we must exist;
> that place is not going to be yielded
> up to us by philanthropy, by charity,
> but only through that stronger power
> that will compel others to give us
> that which is our due. I say POWER
> because it is necessary. Except the
> individual, the race or the nation
> has power that is exclusive; it
> means that that individual, that
> race or that nation will be bound
> by the will of the other who
> possesses this great qualification;
> hence it is advisable for the Negro
> to get power; get power of every

> kind, power in education, in
> science, in industry, in politics,
> in higher government, and physically.
> We want that kind of power that will
> stand out signally so that other
> races and nations can see, and if
> they won't see, feel. POWER is the
> only argument that satisfies man. Man
> is not satisfied; neither is he moved
> by prayers, by petitions, but every
> man is moved by that power of authority
> which forces him to do, even against
> his will . . . The only advice I can
> give the Negro is to get power.[55]

In that sense the salvation/redemption Garvey most
earnestly sought was both social and this--worldly.
He shared with the proponents of the Social Gospel who
were his contemporaries a rejection both of the
overemphasis on salvation of the individual soul and
of another worldly orientation which led to neglect
of man's physical and social needs. For example,
the essence of the Social Gospel movement can be
captured in the final page of Walter Rauschenbusch
publication of his Christianity and the Social Crisis.
He disclosed his vision of God's coming Kingdom in
this manner:

> If at this juncture (the twentieth century)
> we can rally sufficient religious
> faith and moral strength to snap the
> bonds of evil and turn the present
> unparalleled economic and intellectual
> resources of humanity to the harmonious
> development of a true social life, the
> generations yet unborn will mark this
> as that great day of the Lord for
> which the ages waited, and count us
> blessed for sharing in the apostolate
> that proclaimed it.[56]

---

[55]Negro World 12:16 (3 June 1922), p. 1.

[56]Walter Rauschenbusch, Christianity and the
Social Crisis (New York, 1907), p. 422.

Moreover, the Social Gospel was a form of millenial thought; yet it was also an authentic "gospel" bringing good tidings of great joy to the people. Sydney Ahlstrom, the American Historian, characterized the movement in this way:

> The Social Gospel, needless to say, did not consist solely of biblical exegesis and theological elaboration; indeed those are the two elements it most definitely lacked. It was always chiefly concerned to find out the truth about society, and on the basis of that knowledge to chart programs for ameliorating the country's social woes.[57]

Similarly, Garvey, in his passionate demand for social justice, had no illusion that the Kingdom was nearly at hand. He charted a course for the liberation of his people. At the conclusion of a survey of international events, Garvey remarked:

> Those of us who lead the Universal Negro Improvement Association can interpret the signs of the times. We foresee the time when the great white race in America will have grown numerically to the point of selfish race exclusion, when no common appeal to humanity will save our competitive race from their prejudice and injustice, hence the Universal Negro Improvement Association warns the Negro of America as well as of the western world of the dangers of the future, and advises that the best effort of today should be that concentrated on the building up of a national home of our own in Africa.[58]

---

[57]Sydney Ahlstrom, A Religious History of the American People (London, 1972), p. 796.

[58]"Speech of Marcus Garvey . . . August 1st" (1922), p. 16.

Garvey declared that the time had come for the Black race to map out a pathway for themselves in the course of human civilization. He said that the Black race "shall go forward, upward, and onward toward the great goal of human liberty" and that it was his determination that all barriers placed in the way of the progress of the Black race must be removed and cleared away by Blacks themselves, because the light of a brighter day had come. The brighter day, as Garvey perceived it, was the vision of a redeemed African nationality for the Black race:

> Keep your eyes steadfast on the object, and what is it? It is the emancipation of four hundred million souls. It is the freeing of our own country Africa and the making of it of a great United States, a powerful government, not to be controlled by alien races, but to be dominated by ourselves. This is the object, this is the vision, for this we live, and for this we will die . . .
>
> As the war clouds gather let us gird our loins and in greater numbers and stronger determination hold fast until the hour comes, and come it surely will . . . Four hundred million Negroes are ready for the march toward African redemption.[59]

This theme of African redemption served as an important focus for Garvey, and functioned primarily in a religious sense as the eschatological goal toward which all of history was leading. Garvey challenged the Black race to direct all their efforts towards this realization. In one of his many eloquent statements of this theme, Garvey illustrated how the vision of Africa redeemed could empower one to act on his own behalf for the salvation of the race:

> I have a vision of the future, and I see before me a picture of a redeemed Africa, with her dotted cities, with her beautiful civilization, with her

---

[59]_Negro World_ 13:22 (13 January 1923), p. 1.

millions of happy children, going
to and fro. Why should I lose hope,
why should I give up and take a
back place in this age of progress?
Remember that you are men, that God
created you lords of this creation.
Lift up yourselves, men, take yourselves out of the mire and hitch
your hopes to the stars; yea, rise
as high as the very stars themselves.
Let no man pull you down, let no man
pull you down, let no man destroy your
ambition, because man is but your
companion, your equal; man is your
brother; he is not your Lord; he is
not your sovereign master.[60]

On the one hand, when one examines the poems and
anthems Garvey wrote which depict this eschatological
vision of redemption, there is a sense of a cosmic
dimension which will take place in the distant future.
It would appear that God will bring in the Kingdom on
behalf of the Black race. Garvey captured this
concept of the Kingdom inone of his poems, in this
manner:

Out of the clear of God's Eternity
Shall rise a kingdom of Black
Fraternity; There shall be conquests
O'er militant forces; For as man
proposes, God disposes. Signs of
retribution are on every hand,
Be ready, Black men, like Gideon's
band. They may scoff and mock at
you today, But get ready for the
awful fray.

In the fair movement of God's abounding
grace, There is a promised hope for
the Negro race; In the sublimest truth
of prophecy, God is to raise them to
earthly majesty. Princes shall come
out of Egypt so grand, The noble Black
man's home and motherland, The Psalmist

_____

[60]_Negro World_ 12:3 (4 March 1922), p. 1.

spoke in holy language clear,
As Almighty God's triune will declare.

The resplendent raysof the morning sun
Shall kiss the Negro's life again begun;
The music of God's rhythmic natural law
Shall stir Africa's soul without Divine
flaw. The perfume from Nature's rosy
hilltops
Shall fall on us spiritual dewdrops.
Celestial beings shall know us well,
For by goodness, in death with them
we'll dwell.[61]

This theme was continued repeatedly in the National
Anthem which the Convention of the United Negro
Improvement Association authorized for the Black
race to be sung at the opening of each meeting:

Ethiopia, thou land of our fathers,
Thou land where the gods loved to be,
As storm cloud at night sudden gathers
Our armies come rushing to thee.
We must in the fight be victorious,
When swords are thrust outward to gleam;
For us will the victory be glorious
When led by the red, black and green.

Chorus

Advance, advance to victory!
Let Africa be free!
Advance to meet the foe
With the might
Of the red, the black, and green.

Ethiopia, the tyrant's falling
Who smote thee upon thy knees;
And thy children are bustily calling
From over the distant seas.
Jehovah the Great One has heard us,
Has noted our sighs and our tears,
With His spirit of love He has stirred us
To be one through the coming years.

---

[61]Marcus Garvey, The Tragedy of White Injustice
(New York, 1927), pp. 18-19.

Chorus

O Jehovah, Thou God of the ages,
Grant unto our souls that lead
The wisdom Thou Gav'st to Thy sages
When Israel was sore in need.
Thy voice thro' the dim past has spoken,
Ethiopia shall stretch forth her hand,
By thee shall all fetters be broken
And Heaven bless our dear Motherland.[62]

On the other hand, even when denying that his vision of the future was anything more than a careful analysis of political realities, his prophetic self-consciousness was never far from the surface. Garvey had a vision, not a dream. In that sense he was not ahead of his time. It was the Black race that Garvey claimed was dragging for centuries behind the times. This was evident in a speech Garvey delivered as he explained the political program of the United Negro Improvement Association. As Garvey often did, he couched the speech in religious language:

> I am sounding this second warning, and I want you to take it from a man who feels the consciousness of what he says. I am not pretending to be a sage or a philosopher. I am not pretending to be a prophet. I am but an ordinary man with ordinary common sense who can see where the mind blows, and the man who is so foolish as not to be able to see and understand where the wind blows, I am sorry for . . . I can see where the wind is blowing, and it is because of what I see that I am talking to you like this.[63]

---

[62]McGuire, Universal Negro Catechism, pp. 32-33.

[63]Negro World 10:2 (26 February 1921), p. 4.

The wind only bloweth; however, as the gospel writer
tells us, where it listeth, and the one who can discern where it blows is surely a man of God. Garvey
knew which way the wind was moving, and as he declared
in one of his most celebrated passages, its object
was Africa and the goal of salvation/redemption of
the Black race:

> No one knows when the hour of Africa's
> Redemption cometh. It is in the wind.
> It is coming. One day, like a storm,
> it will be here. When that day comes
> all Africa will stand together.[64]

Garvey argued that only when man is able to
expand his conscious awareness of the true God as
Creator and Sovereign Power in his life, and his
relationship to Him as a son of God, that he frees
himself to accept a glorious new life. He contended
that this new life is what Jesus called the Kingdom
of God, and that He taught that the Kingdom of God
is a consciousness of God given dominion over the
things of this world. Garvey challenged the Black
race to realize that the Kingdom of God was right
within them as Jesus taught, and that their salvation/
redemption was assured once they realized they were
heirs to that mighty power which the Creator God
bestowed upon them.

Garvey persistently claimed that within the
Black race was a sovereign power, an authority that
was absolute. He argued that "if Negroes can get
to know themselves, then in the next twenty-four
hours we would have a new race, a new nation,
resurrected, not from the will of others, but our own
will to rise, irrespective of what the world thinks".
Garvey lifted up the innate power and sovereignty
which was a part of all of God's creation, and
declared that the recognition and knowledge of this
force within would ultimately save and redeem the
Black race.

---

[64]Garvey, Philosophy of Opinions, I, p. 10.

Chapter V

GARVEY'S CONTRIBUTION TO BLACK THEOLOGY

It was the brother of the contemporary Black theologian James Cones, Cecil Cone, author of The Identity Crisis in Black Theology, who challenged contemporary Black theologian's to clarify--both for themselves and for others--what black religion is. Dr. Cecil Cone said in the preface of his book:

> The embryonic stage of Black Theology is over; commendations for giving birth to the enterprise and nurturing the baby have been given. As Black Theology has come of age, so must its theologians: further pacification of the Black Theologian can only hurt and thwart the development ofthe black theological enterprise. This is a time for intro-spection and analysis. Before Black Theology can experience further growth, before we can move on to the next stage of development, the Black Theologian must clarify--both for himself and for others--what black religion is. Interpreters of Black Theology must begin to ensure that the theology they present is true to the black religious experience which it purports to indicate and represent.[1]

The attempt of this third section is to go one step further, that is, to present an analysis of the theology of Marcus Garvey in relation to the contemporary Black Theology as presented by the current Black Theologians. In this manner, it is the intention that a historical approach to Black Theology will provide a broader context for the content of Black faith. But first, let us look at Garvey as Theologian.

---

[1]Cecil Wayne Cone, The Identity Crisis in Black Theology (Nashville, 1975), pp. 5-6.

A. GARVEY AS THEOLOGIAN

Garvey has on occasions been characterized as a messianic or at least a charismatic religious figure. He has not been seriously regarded as a religious thinker/theologian, self-consciously endeavoring to construct a coherent view of God, Christ, man, and the world, by which his followers could interpret their historical experience as a people. It can be contended that Garvey may have been the great genius for Black people, but they have not acquired a healthy and mature national consciousness since he appeared among them.

Etymologically, theology implies a discussion about God. God is the object, but grasped by man who has heard Him in His historical, in-the-world revelation. In this sense, all theology is bi-polar, both anthropocentric and theocentric. The theology of Garvey is an attempt to formulate a particular experience, evolving out of Garvey's existential situation in the unfolding of the lives of Black people and their God. To this end, Garvey chose as the central theme of his conscientizational efforts-- the Black race in a decisive moment of their historical process--the slogan, "Up You Mighty Race."

On this base, and in relation to the current Black theologians, a case will be made for viewing Garvey as the pre-eminent Black theologian of the early 20th century. It will also be argued that the rituals, beliefs, and institutional framework he articulated, taken together, constitute the United Negro Improvement Association as a religious movement. This religious movement, of which Garvey was the founder and President, can best be described as a form of Black Civil Religion. For Garvey groped for the creation of the United Negro Improvement Association, and later the African Orthodox Church as an arm of the Association, as a "great Christian Confraternity" which would be expressive of the "conscientious spiritual worship" he perceived as requisite to unification of his people.

The United Negro Improvement Association was by no means only a religious movement; but without appreciating the centrality of its theological dimensions, one cannot fully grasp either the UNIA or its enormous appeal among a wide range of Black

95

people. Garvey sought to cast the UNIA into an all-embracing institution. What he was struggling to institutionalize can most accurately be as a species of civil religion, more specifically a Black civil religion. It provided a common set of shared beliefs and value commitments which sought to bind its adherents--all those men and women of African descent who proudly took the name Negro--into a collectivity which was divinely called to a special task in the world. An unsigned article appearing in the Negro World in August 1923 stated the goal for which Garvey was striving, and from which one can extract Garvey's theology:

> The churches were not doing the work undertaken by Marcus Garvey, yet some preachers are among the crusaders. A full explanation of their attitude might be pretty hard to arrive at and harder to state without lutering on contentions matter. It is enough simply to point out the obvious fact that Negro churches are divided, in some cases forbidden to work together with other movements, and they furnish no convenient meeting--ground for united work. Only a movement that welcome all people of all denominations and is officially attached to none while having its own assembly halls can spread its net wide enough to gather in all people desiring to identify with it.[2]

In this manner, as compared with the current Black theologians, with the exception of Albert Cleage, Garvey adopted an ecclesiology as a channel for the explication of his religious beliefs.

On the one hand, the formation of this channel, this movement, possessed its own meeting halls, its own liturgy as set forth in the Ritual and in the book of Universal Negro Catechism, its distinctive set of beliefs, and even special holidays of its own creation. The beliefs and rituals of the UNIA,

---

[2]Negro World 14:25 (4 August 1923), p. 2.

however, were of a sufficiently high level of
generality so that in assenting to them one could
continue to adhere to particular doctrines and
practices of the separate Black denominations; and
one could still attend those churches on Sunday
mornings while participating in UNIA activities on
Sunday evenings.

On the other hand, there was an element and
subjectivism of mysticism in Garvey's theology which
led Garvey to say:

> You can worship God by yourself. You
> are responsible to God by yourself.
> You have to live your own soul before
> Nobody but yourself can save your
> soul. Others may advise you because
> of your ignorance of life how to
> shape your soul. Keep in communion
> with God. But none can save your
> soul but yourself in your soul
> relation with God.[3]

To make his point even more clear and personal
Garvey urged his hearers to worship with their own
heart, soul and mind, and make their heart, soul or
mind their altar. He expressed it eloquently in
this poem which he wrote entitled "My Altar":

My Altar

I've built a sacred place all mine,
To worship God, who is Divine,
I go there everyday, in thought,
Right to my own, dear sacred heart--

My Altar

No one can change me in my mood,
For I do live on God's sweet food,
He feeds me everyday, with love,
While angels look at it above--

---

[3]Burkett, Black Redemption, p. 40.

My Altar

When all the world goes wrong without,
I never hold one single doubt,
For I do find a great relief--

My Altar

I see the Savior of the world,
Whose light to all has been unfurled,
He utters agonizing plea,
With shining eyes that surely see--

My Altar

I shall remain with faith of rock
To see the Shepherd lead His flock
And when He comes to claim each heart,
My yield shall be in wholesome part--

My Altar[4]

However, the symbols, rituals, and beliefs which
constituted Garvey's Black civil religion, or the
theology of Garvey which this dissertation contends,
were of course not new to Garvey's audience; indeed,
had they been new they would not have found a
responsive hearing. They rather grew out of, and
built upon, a shared experience of slavery, oppression,
and of racial discrimination, as that experience was
interpreted in the light of a transcendent goal:
the uplift of the Black race and the Redemption of
Africa. Garvey served as an inspirer of the Black
race, and set the pace for a new analysis of the
historical experience ofhis people. To this end
Garvey gave his life inone great bid to awaken the
Black race to recognize their inherent power as
creatures created in the image and likeness of God,
the Creator and Sovereign Power.

It should be evident that the characterization
of Garvey as the pre-eminent Black theolgian of the
20th century is one that is being presented not
simply by virtue of the fact that a considerable
number of Garvey's speeches, poems and articles took

---

[4]Ibid., pp. 40-41.

up the subject matter of religion: nor is it being
a source of contention because of Garvey's insistence
on seeing God and Christ through the spectacles of the
Black race, and ultimately through the spectacles of
Ethiopia--the God of Ethiopia. The point is rather
that, in an unsystematic but ne ertheless scientific
and consistent manner, Garvey was doggedly and
untiringly about the business of interpreting the
world and its travails in an ultimately meaningful
way. In an excerpt of an article entitled "Present
Day Civilization" Garvey declared:

> We are circumvented today by
> environments more dangerous than
> those which circumvented other
> peoples in any other age. We are
> face to face with environments in
> a civilization that is highly
> developed; a civilization that is
> competing with itself for its own
> destruction; a civilization that
> cannot last, because it has no
> spiritual foundation; a
> civilization that is vicious, crafty,
> dishonest, inmoral, irreligious and
> corrupt.
>
> We see a small percentage of the
> world's populace feeling happy and
> contended with this civilization that
> man has evolved, and we see the masses
> of the human race on the other hand
> dissatisfied and discontended with
> the civilization of today--the
> arrangement of the human society.
> Those masses are determined to destroy
> the systems that hold up such a society
> and prop such a civilization.
>
> As by indication, the fall will come.
> A fall that will cause the universal
> wreck of the civilization that we now
> see, and in this civilization the Negro
> is called upon to play his part. He
> is called upon to evolve a national

ideal, based upon freedom, human
liberty and true democracy.[5]

An another article entitled "World Readjustment",
Garvey continued the task of interpreting the world
situation for his hearers:

> The political re-adjustment of the
> world means this--that every race
> must find a home; hence the great
> cry of Palestine for the Jews--
> Ireland for the Irish--India for the
> Indians and simultaneously Negroes
> are raising the cry of "AFRICA FOR THE
> AFRICANS", those at home and those
> abroad.
>
> It is a cry for political re-
> adjustment along natural lines, and
> this re-adjustment has come out of
> the war of 1914-18, because, we, as
> Negroes, realize that if (with our
> knowledge and experience of western
> civilization) we allow the world to
> adjust itself politically without
> taking thought for ourselves, we
> would be lost to the world in
> another few decades.[6]

Furthermore, as a means of indicating a transnational
approach to the ideals and principles that Garvey
upheld, in a speech entitled, "Great Ideals Know No
Nationality", he asserted that:

> All intelligent people know that one's
> nationality has nothing to do with
> great ideals and great principles. If
> because I am a Jamaican the Negro should
> not accept the principle of race rights
> and liberty, or the ideal of a free and
> independent race; then you may well say
> that because Jesus was a Nazarene the
> outside world should not accept His

---

[5]Garvey, Philosophy of Opinions, I, p. 31.

[6]Ibid., p. 34.

His Doctrine of Christianity,
because He was an "alien".

Because Martin Luther was born in
Germany, the world should not accept
the doctrine of Protestantism.

Because Alexander Hamilton and
Lafayette were not born in America,
Americans should not accept and
appreciate the benefits they
bestowed upon the nation.

Because Marconi was an Italian, we
of the new world should not make use
of wireless telegraphy. Again I say,
great principles, great ideals know
no nationality.

I know no national boundary where the
Negro is concerned. The whole world is
my province until Africa is free.[7]

Garvey perceived the whole of human civilization
from the perspective of the historical experience of
a people, and the history of a movement, the history
of a nation, the history of a race as a guide-post
of that movement's destiny, that nation's destiny,
that nation's destiny, that race's destiny.

On the one hand, though rejecting any dogmatic
claim concerning the finality of his own perceptions,
Garvey once said:

Religion is one's opinion and belief
in some ethical truth. To be a Christian
is to have the religion of Christ, and so
to be a believer of Mohammed is to be a
Mohemmedan but there are so many religions
that every man seems to be a religion
unto himself. No two persons think
alike, even if they outwardly profess
the same faith, so we have as many
religions in Christianity as we have
believers.[8]

---

[7]Ibid., pp. 36-37.
[8]Ibid., p. 3.

On the other hand, Garvey was convinced of the
indelibly religious nature of man. He insisted on
one level that religion was a phenomenon universally
experienced, and that no man ought to criticize
another either for holding to religion in general or
for believing in a particular conception of the
deity. Speaking at the Sixth International
Convention of the UNIA (1929), Garvey declared:

> Man is a religious being, that is to
> say, he must have some kind of belief--
> call it superstition or what not.
> Man who has started to think traces
> his origin beyond man; and as such
> has been groping in the dark to find
> out the source from whence he came,
> and by our own intuition we have
> attributed that source to something
> beyond us; and in so believing we
> accept the idea of a religion. Some
> make our God the God of Fire; some
> make our God the God of Water; some
> make our God the God of Elements and
> others of us accept the Christian
> belief. Man's religion is something
> we cannot eliminate from his system
> or destroy in him; therefore it is
> folly for any man to go about attacking
> another man's religion, because to him
> it is fundamental. You may be a
> Christian; you may be a Mohammedan;
> that is your religion. We are all
> entitled to our own religious belief.
> Some of us are Catholics, some of us
> are Presbyterians, some of us are
> Baptists, and we deem it a right to
> adhere to our particular belief.[9]

On the same theme, in another speech, Garvey declared:

> It is only the belief and the confidence
> we have in a God why man is able to

---

[9]"Speech of Marcus Garvey Outlining Discussion
on Formulation of Plans to Unify the Religious
Beliefs and Practices of the Entire Negro Race", The
Blackman (Kingston), 31 August 1929, p. 13.

understand his own social institutions,
and move and live like a rational human
being. Take away the highest ideal--
FAITH and CONFIDENCE IN A GOD--and
mankind at large is reduced to savagery
and the race destroyed.[10]

In the final analysis, it was precisely Garvey's
relativism coupled with his ineradicable belief
in the transcendent, which permitted Garvey to have
no qualms about defining God, Christ, Man, Salvation/
Redemption, in the light of the historical experiences
and needs of his own people. However, God was never
the God only of men and women of African descent,
thereby demonstrating the inclusiveness of Garvey's
theology. In advocating that God has no color,
Garvey said:

If the white man has the idea of a
white God, let him worship his God as he
desires. If the yellow man's God is of
his race let him worship his God as he
sees fit.[11]

Yet He was uniquely the God of Ethiopia who had
promised that princes would be brought forth out of
Egypt and into their own heritance. Therefore,
Garvey boldly claimed, the theology of God that
facilitated the religious interpretation of the
historical experience of the Black race:

We, as Negroes, have found a new ideal.
Whilst our God has no color, yet it is
human to see everything through one's
own spectacles, and since the white
people have seen their God through
white spectacles, we have only now
started out (late though it be) to
see our God through our own spectacles.
The God of Isaac and the God of Jacob
let Him exist for the race that believes

---

[10]Garvey, Philosophy of Opinions, I, p. 2.

[11]Ibid., p. 44.

in the God of Isaac and the God of
Jacob. We Negroes believe in the
God of Ethiopia, the everlasting
God—God the Father, God the Son,
and God the Holy Ghost, the One God of
all ages. That is the God in whom
we believe, but we shall worship Him
through the spectacles of Ethiopia.[12]

In this manner he introduced in the early 20th
century a conception of God that facilitated in a
way the goals and aspirations of the Universal Negro
Improvement Association, and developed a rede-
finition of God in the light of Pan-Africanism. It
is to this extent that Garvey could be characterized
as the pre-eminent Black theologian of the 20th century. Granted, the themes were by no means new to
the tradition of the Black Church and the Black
experience; what was distinctive was the uncompromising this—worldly context in which they were
interpreted, and the supra-institutional structure,
anemly the UNIA, into which Garvey sought to organize
them.

---

[12]Ibid., p. 44.

B. GARVEY AND THE CURRENT BLACK THEOLOGIANS

One willfind that Garvey's theology is at variance with the theology of most of the major contemporary Black theologians. Whereas, the emphasis of contemporary Black theology, with the exception of Elijah Muhammad and Albert Cleage, is focused on the Black man as object and victim of his history, and situated within a particular existential and geographic location. For example, the themes of several current Black theologians include: "God of the Oppressed", "Suffering by the Oppressed as a Criterion for Liberation", "Black Religion as a Racial Bond in Times of Stress", "Black Religion as a Compensatory Device", "Non-Violence as a Provision for the Healing or Redemption of the Broken Community", "The Value of a Disinterestedness in One's Culture as a Critical Approach to Theologizing", "Assimilation as a Goal of The Christian Community", "An Explication of and Commitment to Reconciliation Between Blacks and Whites", and therefore "Christ as Liberator of the Oppressed" and "Christ as Reconciler of Oppressor and Oppressed".

In the theology of Garvey, stress is placed on the Black man as subject and hero of his history, and as situated within a trans-national geographic boundary. Garvey's theology also borders on apocalyptic tendencies. For example, the themes of the theology of Garvey include: "God of Equality", "The Mighty God, the Mighty Race", "Black Religion in Relation to both Origin and Goal in Africanism", " Black Religion as a Source of Power in, and Commitment to, African Redemption", "Conscience of Equality", "Suffering as a Duty and Obligation by the Reformer to Improve Human Society", "The Eschatological Vision of a Redeemed Africa", and therefore "Christ as Reformer" and "Christ as Resurrected One."

As was stated in the introduction of the dissertation, the attempt of this portrayal of the theology of Garvey is not to provide a corrective for the contemporary Black theology but to show that Garvey assumed a different posture and point of departure. He began with an unshakable belief in the equality of the human race. This posture formed the crux of his theology.

Garvey took his base for affirming the equality

of the human race in his theology of God as Creator
and Sovereign Power of the entire human race. In
this over-arching view he presented a justificiation
for the redemption of the Black race in the present
age. Garvey pointed to the power that resided in
the Black race as creatures created in the image of
God, and therefore perceived that power as something
pertaining to the divine. It was this inherent
power embodied in the Black race from creation that
Garvey claimed was the impetus of the liberation
process in the Black diaspora.

The contemporary Black theologian James Cone
began his hermeneutical approach to the theology of
God from a different point of departure. He began
with a Christian understanding of God which arose
from the biblical view of revelation--a revelation
of God that took place in the liberation of the
oppressed Israel, and which was completed in God
becoming man in Jesus Christ. Cone contended that
the doctrine of God in Black theology must take its
starting point from the God who is participating in
the liberation of the oppressed of the land, and who
makes Himself known through their liberation:

> This means that whatever is said
> about the nature of God and his
> being-in-the-world must be based on
> the biblical account of God's
> revelatory activity. We are not
> free to say anything we please about
> him. While Scripture is not the
> only source that helps us to recognize
> divine activity in the world, it can-
> not be ignored if we intend to speak
> of the Holy One of Israel.[13]

From this identification with the oppressed to
the point that their experience becomes His, Cone
developed the concept of the blackness of God. He
argued that because Black people have come to know
themselves as Black, and because that blackness is
the cause of their own love of themselves and hatred
of whiteness, God Himself must be known only as He

---

[13]James Cone, A Black Theology of Liberation
(Philadelphia and New York, 1970), p. 116.

reveals Himself in His blackness. Cone stated it
in this manner:

> Because God had made the goal of
> Black people His own goal, Black
> theology believes that it is not
> only appropriate but necessary to
> begin the doctrine of God with an
> insistence of His blackness. The
> Blackness of God had made the
> oppressed condition His own.[14]

Whereas, Garvey referred to the blackness of God
in His Sovereign Power, as a means of affirming the
inherent power which God created in the Black race
by creating him in His own image. Consequently, for
Garvey, the Black race being created in the image of
God is equal to other races. Garvey associated the
blackness of God with that of His power and therefore
related it to the inherent power which resided in
the Black race, to the extent that he developed the
concept of the "Mighty God of the Mighty Race".
Cone instead, equated oppression or oppressed with
blackness and with Black people, and asserted that
knowing God meant being on the side of the oppressed,
becoming one with them, and becoming black with God.
From this concept of blackness Cone developed his
theme the "God of the Oppressed", and approached the
realm of Black theology using an "oppressor-oppressed"
model.

Though Cone acknowledged the doctrine of creation
as a statement that God as Creator means that man is
a creature, and that the Black man's being finds its
source in God, and he is black because God is black--
Cone used this approach as a corollary to the presence
of the oppressor. He pointed out that God, and not
White people is the ground of the Black man's being
in a world in which the oppressor defines right in
terms of whiteness. He further claimed that the
Black man's source for meaning and purpose in the
world is not found in his oppressor but in God Himself. Cone's theology of God undoubtedly addressed
the "oppressor-oppressed" dichotomy. Whereas, Garvey's

---

[14]Ibid., p. 120.

theology of God addressed the anthropological view of the "Conscience of Equality".

In Cone's "oppressor-oppressed" model the meaning of Black Power is defined in terms of the relationship that exists between Blacks and Whites:

> When one group breaks the covenant
> of truth and assumes an exclusive role
> in defining the basis of human relation-
> ship, that group plants the seed of
> rebellion. Black Power means that
> blacks are prepared to accept the
> challenge and with it the necessity
> of distinguishing friends from enemies.[15]

Cone also challenged Whites to redistribute power to Blacks in order to enable them to fight their own battles:

> Working for political, social, and
> economic justice always means a
> redistribution of power. It is a
> kind of power which enables the
> blacks to fight their own battles
> and thus keep their dignity.[16]

Dr. Martin Luther King Jr. preferred not to use the concept Black Power in the liberation process. He regarded the concept as more of a slogan that had negative connotations for the Black race and gave the impression that the issue was black domination rather than black equality. In a discourse with staff members of the Southern Christian Leadership Conference Dr. King stated:

> First, it is necessary to understand
> that Black Power is a cry of dis-
> appointment. The Black Power slogan
> did not spring full grown from the

---

[15]James Cone, <u>Black Theology and Black Power</u> (New York, 1969), p. 26.

[16]<u>Ibid.</u>, p. 55.

head of some philosophical Zeus.
It was born from the wounds of despair
and disappointment. It is a cry of
daily hurt and persistent pain. For
centuries the Negro has been caught
in the tentacles of white power.
Many Negroes have given up faith in the
white majority because "white power"
with total control has left them
empty-handed. So in reality the call
for Black Power is a reaction to the
failure of white power.[17]

However, Dr. King saw some positive aspects of the
concept of power in the Black experience. He understood it as the ability to achieve purpose, and the
strength required to bring about social, political
or economic changes. Like Cone, Dr. King operated
within the context of the "oppressor-oppressed" as it
related to the need to re-distribute power. In
elaborating on the concept of Black Power, Dr. King
said:

Second, Black Power, in its broad and
positive meaning, is a call to Black
people to amass the political and
economic strength to achieve their
legitimate goals. No one can deny
that the Negro is in dire need of
this kind of legitimate power. Indeed,
one of the great problems that the
Negro confronts is his lack of power.
From the old plantations of the South
to the newer ghettos ofthe North,
the Negro has been confined to a life
of voicelessness and powerlessness
. . . There is nothing essentially
wrong with power. The problem is
that in America power is unequally
distributed.[18]

---

[17]Martin Luther King, Jr., Where Do We Go From
Here: Chaos or Community? (New York, 1967), p. 38.

[18]Ibid., pp. 42-43.

He further contended that the call for Black power was a psychological reaction to the oppression of Black people by the slaveowners--a psychological indoctrination that was necessary from the oppressor's viewpoint to make a good slave. This reaction has often led to negative and unrealistic responses, and has frequently brought about intemperate words and actions. Whereas, Garvey's concept of Black power was resident in the Black race as creatures created in the image and Sovereign power of God, and therefore originated from an affirming position of the Black race in human history. Dr. King's concept of Black power was reactionary and arose from a victim orientation:

> Out of the soil of slavery came the psychological roots of the Black Power cry. Anyone familiar with the Black Power movement recognizes that defiance of white authority and white power is a constant theme; the defiance almost becomes a kind of taunt. Underneath it, however, there is a legitimate concern that the Negro break away from "unconditional submission" and thereby assert his own selfhood.[19]

Garvey recognized that power was not a reaction to human depravity but a necessary ingredient of human self-worth. For that reason, Garvey had no qualms of raising the consciousness of Black power as a means of engaging the Black race in their own liberation. Dr. King,however, was reacting to the concept of Black power and argued that the Black race cannot entrust its destiny to a concept/ philosophy born of despair and nourished solely on despair,and to a slogan that could not be implemented into a program. It may be that Dr. King's failure to chart a programmatic course for the Black race occasioned his frustration with the concept of Black power. But Garvey not only espoused the concept of Black power, he outlined a program and challenged the Black race to actively participate in

---

[19]Ibid., p. 46.

their own liberation. Garvey presented an alternative model to that of the "oppressor-oppressed" model from which most of the contemporary Black theologians functioned. He called upon the Black race to acknowledge power as a divine right and a functional tool for human upliftment.

Instead of referring to a relationship with the oppressor, through assimilation or reconciliation, as a means of achieving salvation for the Black race, Garvey advocated African solidarity of the past, present, and future. He recalled that the African race was a mighty race in history, and therefore used the rituals and symbols as a source of hope and a sign of the Black race's ability to contribute to its own destiny.

Garvey's model of the "Conscience of Equality" asserts inherent presence of power--a power that is divine by virtue of the races being created equally in the image of God. That is the reason Garvey used the slogan "Up You Mighty Race" with equal force to Black power.

In the "oppressor-oppressed" model, the oppressor will always have to give to the oppressed power, or the oppressed will have to seize power from the oppressor. In this regards Cone stated:

> If whites do not get off the backs
> of blacks, they must expect that
> blacks will literally throw them
> off by whatever means are at their
> disposal. This is the meaning of
> Black power. Depending on the
> response of whites, it means that
> emancipation may even have to take
> the form of outright rebellion. No
> one can really say what form the
> oppressed must take in relieving their
> oppression. But if blacks are pushed
> to the point of unendurable pain,
> with no option but a violent
> affirmation of their own being,
> then violence is to be expected.[20]

---

[20]Cone, <u>Black Theology and Black Power</u>, p. 22.

In Garvey's model, the Black race asserts power by developing within oneself and within the community the potential power that therein resides in that individual and community. In defining power, Garvey declared:

> Power is the only argument that satisfies men. Except the individual, the race or the nation has POWER that is exclusive, it means that that individual, race or nation will be bound by the will of the other who possesses this great qualification.[21]

He therefore urged Black people to know themselves, to know that in them is a sovereign power, an authority that is absolute, that if they accept a superior human being they accept an insult to the God that is within them.

In Cone's model, when the oppressed gains power it is likely that he will become oppressive because the oppressed can only seize power from a position of solidarity which bespeaks of power in itself, or arrogated power.

Garvey's appeal to recognize the presence of power within the individual and to use that power to reform human society, begins with a self-awareness and an affirmation of self as an instrument of God. This awakening will bring about the redemption of the Black race and ultimately all of humanity. Garvey regarded this goal of redemption, Black Zionism, as a pre-condition for a new humanity among all the races. However, Garvey's primary aim was not to create a "world view" for the human race, but rather to address himself to the particular historical experience of the Black race.

This particularistic view of Garvey with regards to Black Zionism differed sharply from Deotis Roberts' model which sought the salvation/liberation of Black race through reconciliation with the White race. For Roberts, the universality of the Christian

---

[21]Garvey, _Philosophy of Opinions_, I, p. 21.

gospel which requires and produces reconciliation, must be expounded and defended, whatever the cost:

> To many blacks reconciliation will come as harsh judgement. However, the black theologian's role is that of prophet . . . His message will often be unwelcome by blacks as well as whites. But insofar as he speaks the Christian message in the area of race, he will need to speak of reconciliation beyond confrontation and liberation whatever the risk and whatever the personal cost.[22]

The theology of Garvey essentially foster the dis-establishment of the Christian church as a community of all races, and points to the ingathering of the exiles. It is at this juncture that one has to wrestle with his concept of Black Zionism in relation to Roberts' integrative model. Garvey would contend that Black Zionism as a criterion for the new humanity does not negate the co-equal status of all other races in the new humanity or new world order. Garvey's affirmation of Black Zionism provides the message of a liberating gospel, facilitated not by the discovery of something totally new, a new relationship, but through renewal--that is, the creation of a new set of circumstances in keeping with the true origin of man.

Roberts places himself at the opposite extreme from Garvey when he suggests that reconciliation is a necessary goal in the wake of the principle of liberation. He asserts that the task of Black theology is to bring about reconciliation between blacks and whites:

> But as Christians, black and white, we surely know that separation, how-ever rewarding to set the record straight, cannot be an ultimate Christian goal. Separation must give way to reconciliation. The

---

[22]Deotis Roberts, Liberation and Reconciliation (Philadelphia, 1971), p. 22

gospel is a reconciling as well
as a liberating gospel and Christ
is at once Liberator and Reconciler.
At the same time that black Christians
are set free they are called together
with all other Christians, to a ministry
of reconciliation.[23]

Roberts' approach to a Black theology causes
him to experience a definite discontinuity with his
own stated commitment of Black religious tradition
by "sitting loose to religious affirmation" in an
effort to be "open to truth". His approach is in
keeping with his understanding of the academic
tradition, which recognizes the limitations of
"involvement" as insufficiently critical and
evaluative, on the one hand, and sees the value of
"disinterestedness" for critical judgment, on the
other. According to Roberts:

It is possible to study a faith-
claim from the inside, but it is
also possible to understand a faith-
claim from the "outside". The
inside study is too subjective to
be sufficiently critical and
evaluative. The outside study is
more objective and brings a
careful analysis and critical
judgment to bear upon an affirmation
of faith.[24]

While Roberts makes an analysis of the black religious
tradition, his prior commitment to universalism does
not allow a faithful building of his Black theology
upon that foundation.

Whereas, Garvey groped for the creation of a
great Christian Confraternity which would be expressive
of the conscientious spiritual worship he perceived as

---

[23]Ibid., p. 23.

[24]Ibid., p. 26.

114

requisite to the unification of his people. He
commited eis total being to the upliftment/liberation
of the Black race. He even saw his identification
with the Black race in an ontological sense, as he
stated in a speech before incarceration in the
Tombs Prison, June 17, 1923:

> Now, understand me well, Marcus
> Garvey has entered the fight
> for the emancipation of race;
> Marcus Garvey has entered the fith
> fight for the redemption of a
> country. From the grave of
> millions of my forebears at
> this hour I hear the cry, and
> I am going to answer it even
> though hell is cut loose before
> Marcus Garvey. From the silent
> graves of millions who went down
> to make me what I am, I shall
> make for their memory, this fight
> that shall leave a glaring page
> in the history of man. I did
> not bring myself here; they
> brought me from my silent
> repose in Africa 300 years ago,
> and this is only the first
> Marcus Garvey.[25]

Garvey advocated group unity and Black identity as
necessary for the liberation of Blacks, and as a
means of African redemption. His focus was on the
Black race and his ultimate goal was Black Zionism.

In this regard, Garvey led the way for two of
his disciples who fostered a similar thrust in the
early period of the nineteen sixties, namely,
Albert Cleage and Elijah Muhummad. Cleage developed
the concept of Black Zionism through a movement
which he organized and referred to as the Black
Christian Nationalist Movement. Muhammad's concept
of Black Zionism was introduced through the organization of Temples of Islam, and referred to as the
Muslim Movement. He called upon Black people to

25Clarke, _Marcus Garvey and the Vision of
Africa_, p. 150.

"throw off the shackles of the White man's Christianity, and return to Islam, the religion of our ancestors".[26] However, unlike Garvey whose thrust was trans-national, and who lifted up Africa as the Exemplar, Cleage and Muhammad adopted a communal approach, a nation within a nation.

Cleage provided biblical justification for the development of his concept of the Promised Land. In an address to his followers at the Shrine of the Black Madonna in Detroit, Cleage said:

> The Black church can lead Black people to the Promised Land. The Promised Land symbolizes man's eternal dream of a heaven on earth. Our Biblical account begins with Abraham. God spoke to Abraham and sent him out to found a nation. 'I will be your God and you will be mypeople'. Abraham was in Chaldea and God said, 'This is not weere you belong; separate yourself from these people, establish a nation.' The concept of separatism as opposed to integration is a recurring theme in the Old Testament, and God is always on the side of separation. 'You must separate from people who are wrong, who are against you, who are corrupting you, and set up a nation in which you can control your own institutions.' He told Abraham to go out and found a nation? What does it mean to found a nation? It means to go somewhere and begin to set up institutions on which a nation depends. And when God says, 'I will be your God', He means that He will support your efforts with power. This is the history of the Black nation Israelx

---

[26]Elijah Muhammad, <u>Message to The Blackman</u> (Chicago, Illinois, 1965), p. xxiii.

God supported the nation-building process . . . A nation has a right to expect its religious institution to be engaged in the task of building a Promised Land.[27]

He further explained this concept of a Promised Land within the context of the Black experience to mean a nation within a nation as the first step. In emphasizing the communal aspect, Cleage said:

> The Promised Land is a group of people living together and sharing a communal way of life with love for each other. It is not a place but a way of life . . . The Black church has the task of trying to lead Black people to a Promised Land of which many cannot even conceive. This is the first step. Black people must be able to dream of living together with love and dignity, and desire this kind of world for themselves and their children. If we can accept the possibility and desirability of this kind of Black communal living, then we can begin to program for its realization. . . Black Christian Nationalism calls Black people to commit themselves to the possibility of building a Black communal society here on earth by accepting the BCN training and discipline necessary to free the mind from individualism, and materialism and by laboring to restructure the Black church to provide a power base for the systematic building of the Black Nation.[28]

It was obvious that Cleage was very much influenced by Garvey. Therefore, inasmuch as Cleage

---

[27]Albert Cleage, Jr. Black Christian Nationalism (New York, 1972), p. 202.

[28]Ibid., pp. 203-204.

sought to make it possible for the Black church to become relevant to the liberation struggle of Black people in America, he raised the question, 'how ought the Black church to be functioning in the world today?' He projected the concept of Pan-Africanism in keeping with Garvey's concept of 'Ethiopianism' referred to earlier in this dissertation. In defining his program for the Black Christian Nationlist Movement, Cleage stated:

> Our long-term goal is Pan-Africanism, the bringing together of Black people across artificial national boundaries as one people, realizing that we are an African people. No matter where we were taken by the slave ship, we are still an African people. In a very real sense the Black church must substitute the ultimate goal of individual salvation in heaven with God. Pan-Africanism is the objective toward which we struggle. It is the Promised Land for Black people, a Promised Land which includes all Black people in all countries. In addition to the struggle for liberation as Black people wherever we happen to be, it also includes the faith that someday we will reassemble in our home-land Africa.[29]

It is to be noted that Cleage saw Garvey and Muhummad as great leaders of their people who actively engaged in their liberation, and who did not seek validation from, or cooperation with, other groups. In comparing Garvey and Muhummad with other Black leaders, Cleage said:

> So-called Black leaders have been selected by the white oppressor. These Black leaders have been accepted by Black people only in a limited interim capacity, while they waited for integration. Black people have been prepared to delegate

---

[29]Ibid., p. 198.

only limited powers to Black
leaders who shared their Black
inferiority. Only Marcus Garvey
and Elijah Muhammad were given
genuine leadership with power and
authority prior to the emergence
of Black Christian Nationalism with
its centralized authority, rigid
discipline, and fixed body of truth.[30]

Elijah Muhammad's movement developed along
similar lines to that of the Garvey movement, with
the premise that Black people can do for themselves,
and with Black Zionism as its ultimate objective.
In the foreword of Muhammad's book Message to The
Blackman in America, Minister James Shabazz of
Muhammad's Temple of Islam No. 2 Chicago, Illinois,
wrote in 1965:

It has been more than 40 years since
a Negro has appeared on the national
horizon of racial leadership with a
program for his people as contro-
versial and as clear-cut as that of
Elijah Muhammad. Not since the days
of Marcus Garvey, the West Indian
visionary back in 1920, has an
"either or else" plan of Negro
salvation been placed before the
people that is as sharply outlined as
to consequences as that of Muhammad
. . . This is also true of Elijah
Muhammad's Temples of Islam. His
movement is based solidly on
awakening the great masses of
America's 20 million Negroes to the
truth of their racial heritage and
destiny. Like Marcus Garvey, Muhammad
is building his religious group on a
non-white basis and like Garvey has
irrefutable reasons for excluding
whites.[31]

---

[30]Ibid., p. 209.

[31]Muhammad, Message to The Blackman, p. xiii.

In a message to his followers entitled "Build Our Own Society" Muhammad outlined what must be done by the Black race, according to the teachings of Allah:

> You must start thinking and working in the way of independence, as other dependent nations had to do and are still doing, when once free of those who hold you in bondage. Get away from that childish way of thinking that the white man forever owes it to you to provide for you the necessities of life. Should you not be too proud of yourself in this modern time to be thinking in the way of dependence instead of independence? Why are you talking freedom, justice and equality if you do not like to be separated from the people on whom you and your fathers are dependent? Do you think that an independent nation is going to make you it equal while you will not accept your own responsibility to provide for your own? Allah and I want you to be freed of such childish thinking like men and accept responsibility.[32]

His concept of Black Zionism differed from Garvey to the extent that he emphasized the development of a nation within a nation, and focused on Blacks in America:

> A characteristic of Muhammad's teachings is that he never, as Garvey and others did before him, preached "Back to Africa" doctrines as the salvation of the American "so-called Negro". Muhammad says America is not the white man's home; he belongs in Europe and by force took America from "our Asiatic brother, the Indian. We have as much right to this soil as the white man. Why should we

---

[32]Ibid., pp. 301-302.

> claim the land of our Black
> brother in Africa for which
> he has given his life and labor?
> It belongs to him. Our destiny,
> he points out, "is right here in
> America".[33]

It was Muhammad's insistent message that Allah (God) wanted to make a nation out of the Black race, and he challenged Black people, like Garvey his predecessor, to join in a program for a united Black nation. In his theological interpretation of the Son of Man on the Judgment Day, Muhammad declared:

> There are the days of the resurrection
> of the mentally dead so-called Negroes.
> The Son of Man is here. His coming
> has been fulfilled. He seeks that
> which was lost (the so-called Negroes).
> Many now are receiving His name, and
> that name alone will save you. The
> wicked nations of the earth are sorry
> and angry to see the Son of Man set
> up a government of justice and
> peace over this, their wicked
> world . . . We must have a new ruler
> and a new government, where the
> people can enjoy freedom, justice
> and equality. Let the so-called
> Negroes rejoice, for Allah has
> prepared for them what the eye
> has not seen, the ear has not
> heard, and the heart has not been
> able to conceive . . . You have heard
> of old that God prepared a body, or the
> expected Son of Man; Jesus is a
> specially prepared man to do a work
> of redeeming the lost sheep (the so-
> called Negro).[34]

In the same period of the early nineteen sixties two other Black theologians, Joseph Washington, Jr.

---

[33]Ibid., p. xiv.

[34]Ibid., p. 19.

and Dr. Martin Luther King, Jr., espoused a different
approach from Garvey's rallying call of Black Zionism.
Washington advocated the position of assimilation over
against integration as a dynamic concept discribing
the direction of the Black race in the area of
Protestantism and the Christian faith. Dr. King
contended that the liberation of Black people can
only come through integration, the mutual sharing
of power between the oppressed and the oppressor.

In his challenge to both Black and White
Christians, Washington argued that:

> The concept of integration blinds
> both Negroes and Whites to the
> realism that a life apart does not
> lead to a life together . . .
> Assimilation is a mediating con-
> cept--more realistic than inte-
> gration and less provocative than
> miscegenation. If Negroes and
> Whites are to the "one as the
> hand in all things essential to
> mutual progress", a heightened
> sense of assimilation beyond
> integration is the conscious
> process toward this objective.[35]

He contended that this process of assimilation of
Black and White persons can best be accomplished
through the denominational structures of Protestantism.
Whereas Garvey called for the creation of separate
Christian confraternity to fulfill the dreams and
aspirations of the Black race, Washington challenged
the existing structures of the Christian church:

> The creation of this kind of
> climate in the local congregation
> through the organizational proce-
> dures of the denomination is a
> major responsibility. The basis
> for this widespread affirmation
> is the faith that within the
> Christian community there is always
> and everywhere the possibility of

---

[35]Joseph Washington, Jr. Black Religion (Boston,
1964), pp. 260-261.

renewal, while in black religion
the basis for renewal has been
truncated. The possibility for
renewal within the Negro, as within the white Christian, remains
constant but without the community
of faith individual maturation
remains of frustrated potential.
Denominational organizational
machinery can be helpful in pin-
pointing what the congregations are
called upon to do and why.[36]

He also placed the responsibility of this process
of assimilation on the Black race, and specifically
the Black congregations:

The responsibility of all Negro
congregations which exist essentially
because of racial ties is to go out
of business. The total revolution
in which the Negro is involved has
only begun . . . By virtually giving
up their segregated worship life,
old forms in order that new ones might
be reborn would contribute to the
purpose of the church and America.
Were Negroes to be assimilated into
the Christian community, they would
gain much and add new life.[37]

Garvey was definitely opposed to race assimilation.
In an address on this subject Garvey declared:

Some Negro leaders have advanced the
belief that in another few years the
white people will make up their minds
to assimilate their black populations;
thereby sinking all racial prejudice
in the welcoming of the black race
into the social companionship of the

---

[36]Ibid., p. 268.

[37]Ibid., p. 289.

white. Such leaders further believe
that by the amalgamation of the
black and white, a new type will
spring up, and that type will
become the American and West Indian
of the future. This belief is
preposterous. The white man of
America will not, to any organized
extent, assimilate the Negro,
because in so doing, he feels that
he will be committing racial
suicide . . . But when the Negro
by his own initiative lifts himself
from his low state to the highest
human standard he will be in a
position to stop begging and praying,
and demand a place that no individual,
race or nation will be able to deny
him.[38]

Dr. King also differed sharply from Marcus Garvey,
as he called for the creation of a multi-racial
society, and challenged Blacks to join in alliances
with Whites. In an analysis of the concepts of Black
Power and Black Zionism Dr. King said:

In the final analysis the weakness
of Black Power is its failure to
see that the Black man needs the
white man and the white man needs
the black man. However much we
may try to romanticize the slogan,
there is no separate black path
to power and fulfillment that does
not intersect white paths, and
there is no separate white path
to power and fulfillment, short
of social disaster, that does not
share that power with black
aspirations for freedom and human
dignity. We are bound together in
a single garment of destiny. The
language, the cultural patterns,
the music, the material prosperity
and even the food of America are an

---

[38]Garvey, Philosophy of Opinions, Vol. 1, p.26.

amalgan of black and white.[39]

Unlike Garvey who contended that the liberation of Black people was a responsibility that they had to assume for and by themselves, Dr. King, very much rooted in the American context, argued that it was impossible to divide the phenomena of integration and liberation:

> There is no theoretical or sociological divorce between liberation and integration. In our kind of society liberation cannot come without integration and integration cannot come without liberation . . . On the one hand, integration is true inter-group, interpersonal living. On the other hand, it is the mutual sharing of power. I cannot see how the Negro will be totally liberated from the crushing weight of poor education, squalid housing and economic strangulation until he is integrated, with power, into every level of American life.[40]

Dr. King based this concept of integration on his understanding of the principle of love, and therefore extended it to all religious groups within the society:

> This call for a world-wide fellowship that lifts neighborly concern beyond one's tribe, race, class and nation is in reality a call for an all-embracing and unconditional love for all men. This often misunderstood and misinterpreted concept has now become an absolute necessity for the survival of man. When I speak of love, I am speaking of that force which all

---

[39]Martin Luther King, Jr., Where Do We Go From Here: Chaos or Community (New York, 1967) pp. 60-61.

[40]Ibid., p. 71.

the great religions have seen as
the supreme unifying principle of
life. Love is the key that unlocks
the door which leads to ultimate
reality.[41]

Although Dr. King admired Garvey for his ability to
mobilize the masses and his commitment to their
liberation, Dr. King disagreed with his concept of
Black Zionism. Instead, Dr. King argued that in the
struggle for racial justice in a multi-racialsociety
where the oppressor and oppressed are both "at home",
liberation must come through integration. However,
it was Garvey's belief in the Divine injuction that
every man and every race must return to its own
"vine and fig tree", and it was to that extent that
he rallied for the redemption of the Black race in
the form of Black Zionism.

The concept of suffering in Black theology is
varied. Garvey, unlike the contemporary Black
theologians, regarded suffering as being subjective.
It was the individual's experience of suffering for
a cause that Garvey addressed. Whereas, most of the
Black theologians focused on the suffering of the
victim, the oppressed ones. Cone argued from the
position that since Blacks as a people experienced
suffering, God will liberate them. Cleage understood
Black suffering as a badge of shame, and a punishment
for sin, that of failing to resist the oppressor.
Washington contended that the Black man's suffering
is a clue to his chosenness. Dr. King regarded the
suffering of Black people as a tool for creative
dislogue, and as source for the opportunity to inject
new meaning in the veins of American life. In
comparing these theologians with Garvey, one can
detect Garvey's focus on the Black race as subjects
of their history attempting to carve out their
liberation. In his first message to the Blacks of
the world from Atlanta Prison on February 10, 1925,
Garvey said:

My work is just begun, and when the
history of my suffering is complete,
then future generations of Negroes
will have in their hands the guide

---

[41]Ibid., p. 221.

by which they shall know the "sins"
of the twentieth century . . .
After my enemies are satisfied, in
life or death I shall come back to
you to serve even as I have served
before. In life I shall be the
same: in death I shall be a terror
to the foes of Negro liberty. If
death has power, then count me in
death to be the real Marcus Garvey
I would like to be. If I may come
in an earthquake, or a cyclone, or
plague, or pestilence, or as God
would have me, then be assured that
I shall never desert you and make
your enemies triumph over you.
Would I not go to hell a million
times for you?

If I die in Atlanta my work shall then
only begin, but I shall live, in the
physical or spiritual sense to see
the day of Africa's glory. When I
am dead wrap the mantle of the Red,
Black and Green around me, for in the
new life I shall rise with God's
grace and blessing to lead the millions
up the heights of triumph with the
colors that you well know. Look for
me in the whirlwind or the storm, look
for me all around you, for, with God's
grace, I shall come and bring with me
countless millions of black slaves
who have died in America and the West
Indies and the millions in Africa to
aid you in the fight for liberty,
Freedom and Life.[42]

Garvey was glad to suffer and even die in the great
cause of the liberation and redemption of the Black
race. Unlike most of the contemporary Black theologians Garvey's commitment was total. He was a
functional theologian, working out his theology in
praxis.

---

[42]Clarke, *Marcus Garvey and the Vision of
Africa*, p. 190.

In Garvey's theology suffering was understood
as suffering for a cause--the attempt to liberate
the Black race. Whereas, Cone saw suffering in itself
as a criterion for liberation, not suffering a
person is experiencing but the wrong that the
oppressor is inflicting that gives the right to
salvation. As Cone puts it:

> Our loyalty belongs only to Him
> who has become like us in every-
> thing, especially blackness. To
> take seriously the Lordship of
> Christ or his Sonship or Messiah-
> ship is to see Him as the sole
> criterion for authentic existence.
> If He is the Suffering Servant of
> God, He is an oppressed man who has
> taken on that very form of human
> existence that is responsible for
> human misery. What we need to ask
> is this: "What is the form of
> humanity that accounts for human
> suffering in our society? What
> is it, except blackness . . . Is
> it possible to talk about suffering
> in America without talking about
> the meaning of blackness?"[43]

Cone's concept of suffering in Black theology is a
state or condition of the victim. Whereas, Garvey's
concept of suffering was focused on the hero, the
subject of his history, the one who rebelled and
fought for the cause of liberation. Garvey pointed
to suffering only as a life-style for a cause.
Garvey combined the theme of Christ the One who
suffers and Christ the Great Reformer as parts of
whole:

> If we could see the sufferings of
> Christ, if we could see the patience
> of Christ, if we could see the very
> crucifixion of Christ, then we would
> see the creature, the being spiritual
> that God would have us to be . . . He

---

[43] Cone, A Black Theology of Liberation,
pp. 217-218.

was called to yield up that life
for the cause He loved--because
He was indeed a great reformer.[44]

Garvey did not sound off suffering as a state or
condition of a people, or a compensatory device,
but pointed to the other side of the polarity--the
strength and power of the Black race.

Cleage picked up on this same theme of suffering,
but as a badge of shame, and challenged Blacks to
throw off the shackles of their suffering:

>Our relationship with God as Black
>men also makes special demands upon
>us. God is disgusted with us because
>we have crawled too long. God did
>not intend for us to accept slavery
>and oppression for almost four
>hundred years. God has been ashamed
>of us for those four hundred years.
>God demands that we fight, that we
>throw off the shackles of bondage
>now; that we stand up as free men
>now; that we come together as black
>brothers now, in the cause of black
>freedom. We must fight, and die if
>need be, that black people may be free
>with the power to stay free. This is
>what God demands of black men.[45]

Cleage even went further by describing suffering as
a punishment for sin. In recounting the faithlessness
of Israel in the Bible, Cleage drew an analogy to
the Black experience of suffering in America:

>We've been oppressed, we've been
>downtrodden. We've been deprived.
>And that is true. But the people who
>accept oppression, who permit them-
>selves to be downtrodden, those people

---

[44]Garvey, _Philosophy of Opinions_, II, pp. 28-30.

[45]Cleage, _The Black Messiah_, pp. 112-113.

are faithless because God did not
make men to be oppressed and to be
downtrodden. And many times a man
faces the choice between living as
a slave and dying as a man. And
when we choose to live as slaves, we
are faithless and our children will
be shepherds in the wilderness.[46]

Against this Biblical imagery and history both
Cleage and Washington raised the question of suffering
of the chosen people in reference to the Black race.
Thus Washington said:

As a result of this suffering by a
whole people for four centuries and
placed in the perspective of the
Bible, we contend here that the Negro
cannot be understood or understand
himself except as another "chosen
people."[47]

Cleage made a similar claim as follows:

We believe in the doctrine of Black
Power as a religious concept revealed
to us, as God's chosen people, in the
Old Testament and in the teachings of
Jesus.[48]

And in another passage he stated:

Perhaps if we could just remember
that we are God's chosen people,
that we have a covenant with God,
then we would know that God will
not forsake us. Even in the midst
of violence and oppression, we would

---

[46]Ibid., pp. 267-268.

[47]Joseph R. Washington, Jr., The Politics of
God (New York, 1969), p. 155.

[48]Cleage, The Black Messiah, p. 274.

know that we are God's chosen
people.[49]

Garvey did not dwell on the theme of chosenness
of Blacks in suffering, which created a pretension
that suffering is okay because God can bring good
out of suffering; or that suffering is okay because
God is Christ identifies with the oppressed. Rather,
Garvey characterized suffering as a life-style
adopted by the individual in his quest for the
liberation of the Black race. With regards the role
of the sufferer, Garvey differed from Dr. King in
the sense that Dr. King called for a passive response
as a dissenter. He was also advocating this role on
behalf of the oppressor and oppressed in the larger
society. Dr. King stated his position in calling
the Black race to integrate integrate into all the
existing values of American history, he said:

> Let us be those creative dissenters
> who will call our beloved nation
> to a higher destiny, to a new
> plateau of compassion, to a more
> noble expression of humaneness.
>
> We are superbly equipped to do this.
> We have been seared in the flames of
> suffering. We have known the agony
> of being the underdog. We have
> learned from our have-not status
> that it profits a nation little
> to gain the whole world of means
> and lose the end, its own soul.
> We must have a passion for peace
> born out of wretchedness and the
> misery of war. Giving our ultimate
> allegiance to the empire of justice,
> we must be that colony of dissenters
> seeking to imbue our nation with the
> ideals of a higher and nobler order.
> So in dealing with our particular
> dilemma, we will challenge the nation
> to deal with its larger dilemma.[50]

---

[49]Ibid., pp. 53-54.

[50]King, Where Do We Go From Here: Chaos or
Community?. pp/ 157-158.

131

Garvey emphasized the role of Christ as Reformer
and the Resurrected One who gives new life. In this
way, he did not dwell on the theme of the chosenness
of Blacks in suffering which creates a pretension
that suffering is okay because Gad can bring good
out of suffering,or that suffering is okay because
God in Christ identifies with the oppressed,
according to Cone. Rather, Garvey characterized
Christ like all great reformers, and presented Him
as a model, one who was radical, rough,unyielding,
uncompromising, and fearing only God. Garvey
declared:

> All true warriors know no fear. Our
> friends are fainthearted, but Jesus
> Christ was the greatest radical the
> world ever saw. Jesus opposed
> wrong. His program was to lift up
> humanity, and save mankind.[51]

Cone, however, lifted up Jesus' Suffering Servant role
as crucial for the liberation of the Black race,
and identified this role with the concept of blackness. As Cone stated in his Christological formulation of the Black Christ:

> If he is the Suffering Servant of
> God, he is an oppressed man who
> has taken on that very form of human
> existence that is responsible for
> human misery. What we need to ask
> is this: "What is the form of
> humanity that accounts for human
> suffering in our society? What
> is it except blackness? If Christ
> is truly the Suffering Servant of
> God who takes upon himself the
> suffering of his people, thereby
> re-establishing the covenant of
> God, then he must be black.[52]

---

[51]Negro World 11:25 (4 February 1922), p. 9.

[52]Cone, A Black Theology of Liberation,
pp. 217-218.

In another passage, Cone defined Christ as the
Oppressed One in order to validate His presence
among the oppressed Black race:

> The definition of Christ as black
> is crucial for Christology if we truly
> believe in his continued presence
> today. Taking our clue from the
> historical Jesus who is pictured
> in the New Testament as the
> Oppressed One, what else, except
> blackness, could adequately tell
> us the meaning of his presence
> today? Any statement about Christ
> today that fails to consider black-
> ness as the decisive factor about
> his Person is a denial of the New
> Testament message.[53]

With regards the concept of the Black Christ,
Garvey argued that Christ had to be conceived
historically as a Black man, not on the basis of his
suffering condition, but genealogically in terms of
her African descent. In one of his Lesson Guides
Garvey emphasized this theme of the blackness of
Christ:

> In reading Christian literature and
> accepting the doctrine of Jesus
> Christ lay special claim to your
> association with Jesus and the Son
> of God. Show that whilst the white
> and yellow worlds, that is to say--
> the worlds of Europe and Asia Minor
> persecuted and crucified Jesus the
> Son of God, it was the black race
> through Simon the Black Cyrenian
> who befriended the Son of God and
> took up the Cross and bore it
> alongside of Him up to the heights
> of Calvary. The Roman Catholics,
> therefore, have no rightful claim
> to the Cross nor is any other pro-
> fessing Christian before the
> Negro. The Cross is the property
> of the Negro in his religion

-----

[53]Ibid., p. 214.

because it was he who bore it.
Never admit that Jesus Christ
was a white man, otherwise he
could not be the Son of God and
God to redeem all mankind. Jesus
Christ had the blood of all races
in his veins, and tracing the
Jewish race back to Abraham and to
Moses, from which Jesus sprang
through the Jesse, you will find
Negro blood everywhere, so Jesus
had much of Negro blood in him.[54]

On this same theme of the Black Christ, Cleage
went one step further than Garvey and traced the
actual blood line of Jesus. He emphatically declared
that Jesus was born to a Black woman Mary, and
therefore was Black. In his book entitled Black
Messiah, Cleage wrote:

Jesus came to the Black Nation Israel.
We are not talking now about "God
the Father". We are concerned here
with the actual blood line. Jesus
was born to Mary, a Jew of the tribe
of Judah, a non-white people; black
people in the same sense that the
Arabs were black people, in the same
sense that the Egyptians were
black people. Jesus was a Black
Messiah born to a black woman . . .
Jesus as a Black Messiah is an
historic fact.[55]

Joseph A. Johnson, Jr., a Black theologian and
Bishop of the Christian Methodist Episcopal Church
emphasized the need for the portrayal of a Black
Messiah. However, he took a more pragmatic and
functional view than that of Garvey and several of

---

[54]Marcus Garvey, Intelligence, (mimeographed),
p. 11.

[55]Cleage, Black Messiah, p. 42.

the other Black theologians. Johnson argued that the tragedy of the interpretations of Jesus by white American theologians during the last three hundred years is that Jesus has been too often identified with the oppressive structures and forces of the prevailing society. Hence the quest, via black consciousness, is for a Black Messiah:

> The world of white theologians is severely limited. This severe limitation of the white theologians' ability to articulate the full meaning of the Christian faith has given rise to the development of black theology . . . But Blacks must "detheologize" their minds in order to recover the essential humanity of Jesus, for the white Christ of the white church establishment is the enemy of the black man. To be a Christian, is to join Christ at the crossways of the world, to participate in His ministry of love and liberation.[56]

Another Black theologian Dr. Howard Thurman ignored the differences of form and color in relation to Jesus Christ, and pointed to the essential spiritual unity which exists between Jesus and the universal man. Thurman declared:

> I affirm my need for a growing understanding of all men as sons of God, and seek after a vital interpretation of God as revealed in Jesus of Nazareth whose fellowship with God was the foundation of His fellowship with men.[57]

In another passage he endeavored to portray a non-

---

[56]C. Eric Lincoln, The Black Experience in Religion, (Garden City, New York, 1974), pp. 126-127.

[57]Howard Thurman, Footprints of a Dream (Harper & Row, New York, 1959), p. 52.

segregated community of worship in which Jesus is
reflected in the life of the individual person:

> Jesus is not Jesus Christ the Son
> of God, but a man everyone meets who
> seeks God. Men come to God through
> nature; it has been said, men may
> come to God through other good men;
> but he who seeks God with all of
> his heart will someday on his way
> meet Jesus.[58]

Although Garvey's view of Jesus Christ included
a principled universalism which demonstrated his
capacity to redeem all of mankind, Garvey differed
from the above mentioned Black theologians in his
attempt to portray Jesus as One who had the blood
of all races in his vein. It was this particularistic interpretation of Christ's significance that
provided Garvey's Black Christ as distinct from the
contemporary Black theologians interpretation of
Jesus Christ for the Black experience. Garvey
balanced the model of Jesus as Suffering Servant with
the model of Jesus as Great Reformer who suffered
death it is true, but who did not do so meekly.
Garvey's aim was to show the power of a righteous
cause.

Garvey developed categories for his theology
from a biblical framework, and used primitive
African society as the Exemplar for the future
resurrection of the Black race. Garvey attempted to
reclaim a secular version of redemption and wholeness,
and integrate it back into biqlical perspective in
order to present it afresh for Black people of his
day. The attempt was to reconnect the fallen state
of the Black race in their present historical
experience with that of the self-affirming state of
the Black race in their past historical experience,
using Africa as the Exemplar.

Garvey also drew symbols and beliefs from the
shared experience of slavery and "Africanism", and
interpreted that experience in the light of a

---

[58]Howard Thurman, Deep is the Hunger (Harper &
Row, New York, 1951), p. 176.

transcendent goal: the upliftment of the Black
race and the redemption of Africa. Garvey's aim
was to recover the African and biblical dimension of
a contemporary existential experience confronting
the Black race by presenting them a vision of self-
past, present, and future. Therefore, he used
categories in his theology in keeping with the
historical experience of the Black race, and rooted in
his understanding of the Black man as the supreme
lord of creation, potentially good and mighty.

Albert Cleage adopted a similar approach to that
of Garvey by using biblical categories and African
concepts to interpret the Black experience. Cleage
interpreted Jesus to have been a Black revolutionary
leader who was seeking to lead a Black nation to
liberation and freedom. He maintained that the
historic roots of the Black church must be recaptured.
He regarded the Black power movement in the 1960's
as a means of raising a Black nationalistic
perspective, and sought to synthesize or create a
union between nationalism and Christianity. It was
his contention that the Black community was prepared
to worship a Black Jesus, and therefore declared:

> Basic to our struggle and the
> revitalization of the Black Church
> is the simple fact that we are
> building a totally new self-image.
> Our rediscovery of the Black
> Messiah is a part of our redis-
> covery of ourselves. We could
> not worship a Black Jesus until
> we had thrown off the shackles
> of self-hate. We could not follow
> a Black Messiah in the tasks of
> building a Black Nation until we
> had found the courage to look
> back beyond the slave block and
> the slave ship without shame.[59]

In his efforts to present Jesus as the Black Messiah,
Cleage was attempting to help Black people view
Jesus in their own image. He believed that only
this kind of focus on the concept of the Black

---

[59]Cleage, Jr., The Black Messiah, p. 7.

137

Messiah would be capable of unifying the Black community around liberation. He saw the Black church as the rallying point to unite all Black people to labor and sacrifice in the spirit of the Black Messiah.

Cleage, like Garvey, tied in the building of the Black Christian church with that of the building of the Black nation. Cleage sought to build a Black nation on the symbol of the Black Madonna and child which would represent the future of the Black nation. It was his position that Black people must take the initiative toward building a nation, as opposed to waiting for God to intervene.

With reference to the concept of the resurrection of Jesus, Cleage's thought paralleled Garvey's with regards to the relationship between the resurrected Jesus and the resurrection of the Black race. Garvey called upon the Black race to view the resurrection of Jesus as the guide to their own resurrection--a resurrection from the lethargy of the past, the sleep of the past, from that feeling that made them accept the idea and opinion that God intended that they should occupy an inferior place in the world. In an Easter message before the Universal Negro Improvement Association, Garvey said:

> Today as we think of our Risen Lord
> may we not also think of the life
> He gave to us--the life that made
> us His instruments, His children--
> The life that He gave to us to make
> us possessors of the land that He
> himself created through His Father.
> How many of us can reach out to
> that higher life; that higher purpose--
> that on this anniversary of our Risen
> Lord, we ourselves will be risen from
> the slumber of the ages; risen in
> thought to higher ideals, to a
> loftier purpose, to a truer con-
> ception of life.[60]

Cleage viewed the concept of the resurrection of

---

[60]Garvey, Philosophy of Opinions, Vol. 1, p. 88.

Jesus, in terms of the raising of the Black consciousness from slave mentality to a new sense of
selfhood, peoplehood, and nationhood. Cleage wrote:

> So the Resurrection that we celebrate
> is not the Resurrection of the
> physical body of Jesus, but the
> Resurrection of the Black Nation
> which He started, the Resurrection
> of His ideas and His teachings.
> The immortality which Jesus has
> lies in the fact that two thousand
> years later we remember, and two
> thousand years later we try to do
> the same thing he tried to do with
> the Black Nation in Palestine.
> Today, in the midst of corruption,
> we are drawing people one by one,
> two by two, into the Black Nation.
> This task and the faith that it
> can be done, this is the Resur-
> rection in many ways.[61]

The concept of Pan-Africanism was a point of
reference as well for Cleage. In outlining the
program of the Black church, Cleage declared:

> Our long-term goal is Pan-Africanism,
> the bringing together of Black people
> across artificial national boundaries
> as one people, realizing that we are
> an African people. No matter where
> we were taken by the slave ship, we
> are still an African people. In a
> very real sense the Black church
> must substitute the ultimate goal
> of Pan-Africanism of individual
> salvation in heaven with God. Pan-
> Africanism is the objective toward
> which we struggle. It is the
> Promised Land for Black people, a
> Promised Land which includes all
> Black people in all countries. In
> addition to the struggle for
> liberation as Black people wherever

---

[61]Cleage, Jr., The Black Messiah, p. 99.

we happen to be, it also includes
the faith that someday we will
reassemble in our homeland,
Africa.[62]

There were other Black theologians who confined
their interpretation of the Black experience to the
American society, and adopted democratic and
Christian theories to substantiate their views.
Among the Black theologians who did not look towards
Africa, but challenged Blacks to assimilate in the
American context, was Joseph Washington. He contended
that the failure of the Christian Church to include
the struggle of the Black man deprived him of a sense
of the universal, as surely as American democracy
has deprived him of his basic rights. Washington
placed the Black struggle in the context of the
American society, and unlike Garvey, challenged the
Black race to assimilate into, and assume responsibility for, the whole of society. Washington
challenged Black Americans to demand assimilation in
the Christian community instead of looking towards
Africa, and added that:

> The choice between being a part of
> the whole or attempting to be a whole
> apart is the decision of the Negro.
> It is within his power to begin
> the long process of assimilation
> into the Christian community and
> therefore the American society,
> from strength, declaring not that
> he wishes to have what the white
> community has nor his intention to
> be like white people; rather, his
> declaration must be that alone and
> separated, white and black America
> are antagonists of the American
> dream and the Christian community.[63]

It was Washington's view that if Blacks were to be

---

[62]Cleage, Jr., Black Christian Nationalism,
p. 198.

[63]Washington, Jr., Black Religion, p. 291.

assimilated into the Christian community and therefore the American society they would gain much and
add new life.

Garvey's use of Africa as the Exemplar provided
an eschatological perspective that was different
from James Cone. For example, Cone contended that
the proper eschatological perspective must be
grounded in the historical present, and therefore,
like Washington, he called upon Blacks to challenge
the present order in the American context. Both
Garvey and Cone repeatedly denounced those who called
for renunciation of the present world and its veil
of woes in favor of a life to come, and those who
encouraged Blacks to forget about present injustice
and look forward to heavenly justice. However, they
differed in their understanding of the concept of
the Promised Land in relation to the liberation of
the Black race.

For Garvey, the theme of the Promised Land was
the "redemption of Africa". This idea of the
"redemption of Africa" functioned primarily in a
religious sense as the eschatological goal toward
which all of history was leading, and for the
realization of which all of one's efforts ought to
be directed. In one of his many eloquent statements
of this theme, Garvey illustrated how the vision of
Africa redeemed could empower one to act on his own
behalf for the upliftment of the Black race:

> I have a vision of the future, and
> I see before me a picture of a
> redeemed Africa, with her dotted
> cities, with her beautiful
> civilization, with her millions
> of happy children, going to and
> fro. Why should I lose hope, why
> should I give up and take a back
> place in this age of progress?
> Remember that you are men, that
> God created you Lords of this
> creation. Lift up yourselves,
> men, take yourselves out of the
> mire and hitch your hopes to the
> stars; yes, rise as high as the
> very stars themselves. Let no
> man pull you down, let no man
> destroy your ambition, because
> man is but your companion, your

equal; man is your brother; he is
not your Lord; he is not your
sovereign master.[64]

Cone's theme of the Promise Land and his attempt to
deal with the question of eschatology in Black
theology was very much rooted in the historical
past as well as present experience of the Black race
in the American context. Cone argued that no
eschatological perspective was sufficient which did
not challenge the present order, and he declared
that Black Americans know all about pearly gates,
golden streets and long white robes:

> We have sung songs about heaven
> until we were hoarse, but it did
> not change the present state or ease
> the pain. To be sure, we may "walk
> in Jerusalem jus' like John" and
> "There may be a great camp meeting
> in the Promised Land", but we
> want to walk in this land--"the
> land of the free and the home of
> the brave". We want to know why
> cannot Harlem become Jerusalem
> and Chicago the Promised Land?[65]

On the one hand, Cone, adopting the "oppressor-
oppressed" model, called upon the oppressed community,
Black Americans, to say NO to unjust treatment
because their humiliation was inconsistent with their
promised future. On the other hand, Garvey articulated a vision of the future towards which his people
could look with expectation and hope. For Garvey,
this theme of the "redemption of Africa" was more than
an image. It was a legitimate political goal, and
a specific objective of the United Negro Improvement
Association. Garvey used the beliefs and symbols
of "Africanism" to bind the Black race in America
into a single people whose task was to build up a
nation in Africa capable firstly of securing that
continent's freedom, and secondly of ensuring the

---

[64]Negro World 12:3 (4 March 1922), p. 1.

[65]Cone, A Black Theology of Liberation, p. 241.

142

rights of Black people wherever they might reside
in the world. In one of his famous speeches,
Garvey said:

> No one knows when the hour of
> Africa's Redemption cometh. It
> is in the wind. It is coming.
> One day, like a storm, it will be
> here. When that day comes all
> Africa will stand together.[66]

Mordecai Johnson, former President of Howard
University and Black theologian also addressed the
question of eschatology and the Black experience
from the perspective of the American political,
educational, economic, cultural and social conditions.
His emphases were not on the traditional notion of
"pie in the sky by and by" or "when we get over
yonder, everything will be all right" kind of
theology. Rather his empases were geared towards
the realization of peace, brotherhood, love, justice,
and liberation here in America. Johnson's concept
of eschatology in relationship to Black Americans
historically, was based on belief in the love and
providence of a just and holy God, belief in the
principles of democracy and the righteous purpose
of the federal government, and belief in the ultimate
disposition of the country. Johnson had faith in
America, and because of this, he was able to look
beyond the cruelty of Black suffering toward an
eschatological future of genuine freedom and
liberation in this world.

It was Johnson's view that America would conquer
all the inhibitions associated with Blackness and
create an atmosphere conducive to an interdependent
relationship between Blacks and Whites. Unlike
Garvey, Johnson saw the realization of the Black
man's liberation in the American context despite the
fact of oppression slavery and racism, and maintained
his faoth in America. He referred to the future
destiny of Black people in these terms:

> I do not conceal my hope, that this
> destiny will be entire public equality

66Garvey, Philosophy of Opinions, I, p. 10.

and entire good-willed cooperative
relations with every element of the
American population, and that he
will be especially understood by
those men who have been his former
masters and who have been accustomed
to make him a slave.[67]

Johnson contended that although America made every
attempt to erase from the minds of Black Americans
all visions of the achievement of independence and
self-respect, the faith of the Black Americans was
grounded in the historic struggle, pain, and prayer
which led to their flight toward freedom and
liberation.

Deotis Roberts, like Cone, emphasized that
eschatology in Black theology must begin with the
present. In other words, Roberts contended that
promise of future awards or punishments make little
impression. He declared:

For Black Christians realized
eschatology, the manifestation
of the will of God in the present,
abstractly as social justice and
concretely as goods and services
to humanize life, must be a first
consideration for a doctrine
pointing to the eventual consum-
mation of God's purposes in
creation and history.[68]

However, Roberts added that eschatology for Blacks
must be both realized and unrealized, and based this
hope in the resurrection of Jesus Christ. In this
regard he differed from Garvey, in that he approached
the vision of the future for the Black race without using any motivating myths in the Black American
and African religious history. He addressed the

---

[67]Inaugural Address of Mordecai Wyatt Johnson,
President, Howard University, June 10, 1927,
"Education for Freedom", Moorland-Spingarn Research
Center, Washington, D.C., 1976, p. 30.

[68]Roberts, Liberation and Reconciliation: A
Black Theology, pp. 156-157.

theme of eschatology from the perspective of the
Christian hope based upon the resurrection of
Jesus Christ:

> The survival and triumph of the hol-
> istic self, of the personality, is
> assured for those who have a saving
> relationship with Christ whom God
> has raised from the dead and has
> "made both Lord and Christ".
> This Christocentric view of the
> resurrection is founded upon the
> faith of Christians in the crucifixion--
> resurrection event. It is based
> upon the faith that the Christian
> shares the passion, cross, and
> power of the Lord of Life and
> Lord over death. Faith in the
> Christus Victor, "the victorious
> Christ", is the basis of our hope,
> as blacks, that both liberation
> reconciliation are assured and
> that meaning and the quest for
> social justice are proper goals
> for our lives.[69]

Garvey's perspective of hope based upon the
resurrection of Jesus Christ was translated in terms
of the call for an inner resurrection of the Black
race. In regards to the significance of the
Resurrection of Jesus Christ as it related to the
hope which Garvey saw for his people, he said:

> As Christ triumphed nearly two
> thousand years ago over death and
> the grave, as He was risen from
> the dead, so do I hope that
> 400,000,000 Negroes of today
> will triumph over the slavishness
> of the past, intellectually,
> physically, morally and even
> religiously; that on this anni-
> versary of our risen Lord, we
> ourselves will be risen from the
> slumber of the ages; risen in

---

[69]Ibid., p. 174.

145

> thought to higher ideals, to a
> loftier purpose, to a truer con-
> ception of life. It is the hope
> of the Universal Negro Improvement
> Association that the 400,000,000
> Negroes of the world will get to
> realize that we are about to live
> a new life--a risen life--a life
> of knowing ourselves.[70]

Garvey's eschatological perspective differed from
the contemporary Black theologians in that he called
upon the Black race to have an ontological identification with the resurrected Christ. But Garvey
was also very practical in his approach as he
challenged the Black race to function in the world
as the lords of creation:

> All that you see in creation, all
> that you see in the world, was
> created by God for the use of man,
> and you four hundred million
> black souls have as much right
> to your possession in this world
> as any other race.
>
> Created in the image of the same
> God we have the same common rights,
> and today I trust that there will
> be a spiritual and material
> resurrection among Negroes every-
> where; that you will lift your-
> selves from the doubts of the past;
> that you will lift yourselves from
> the slumbers of the past, that you
> will lift yourselves from the
> lethargy of the past, and strike
> out in this new life--in this
> resurrected life--to see things
> as they are.[71]

---

[70]Garvey, Philosophy of Opinions, I, p. 88.

[71]Ibid., p. 90.

Garvey groped within the Black experience, and with a vision of the future embodied in the theme of the "Redemption of Africa", he illustrated how the resurrection of Jesus Christ can offer hope to, and empower, the Black race to rise as high as the very stars themselves.

An understanding of the Black church was a matter of considerable concern to Marcus Garvey. Given the fragmentation of the Black churches and the loyalty to the Black churches which the Black clergy and laity exemplified, it was clear that the Universal Negro Improvement Association could never succeed as simply one more denomination or sect from which one might choose one's religious affiliating. Therefore, Garvey strove to avoid the untenable position of forcing his followers to choose between the Universal Negro Improvement Association, which he regarded as a great Christian Confraternity, and a particular Black denomination.

An unsigned article appearing in the Negro World in August 1923 stated the goal for which Garvey was striving in terms of his understanding of the Black church:

> The churches were not doing the
> work undertaken by Marcus Garvey,
> yet some preachers are among the
> crusaders. A full explanation
> of their attitude might be pretty
> hard to arrive at and harder to
> state without entering on contentious
> matter. It is enough simply to
> point out the obvious fact that
> Negro churches are divided, in
> some cases forbidden to work
> together with other movements,
> and they furnish no convenient
> meeting ground for united work.
> Only a movement that welcomes
> all people of all denominations
> and is officially attached to
> none while having its own assembly
> halls can spread its net wide
> enough to gather in all people

desiring to identify with it.[72]

Within this concept of the role of the Universal Negro Improvement Association Garvey sought to bind the Black race into a collectivity which was divinely called to a special task in the world. What Garvey was struggling to institutionalize can most accurately be described as a species of civil religion, more specifically a Black civil religion. It provided a common set of shared beliefs and value commitments which grew out of and built upon a shared experience of slavery and of racial discrimination. For Garvey, this experience was interpreted in the light of a transcendent goal: the uplift of the Black race and the Redemption of Africa. The symbols, rituals, and beliefs which constituted the basis for the Black civil religion were, of course, not new to Black people; indeed, had they been new they would not have found a responsive hearing. They stood as symbols of national solidarity that endeavored to bind the Black race into a single unit, whom God has specially chosen for the task of building up a nation in Africa.

Garvey sought to clarify the Universal Negro Improvement Association's position in relationship to the Black church with the following remarks:

> It was not the desire, he explained, of the Universal Negro Improvement Association to dictate any one's religious faith or religious belief; that was to say, we were not assuming to tell any one to become a Catholic or Baptist or Episcopalian or Seventh Day Adventist or Holy Roller or anything else. The idea was to bring to the Negro a scientific understanding of religion. What was desired was one great Christian confraternity without regard to any particular denomination, believing ourselves to be religious Christians.[73]

---

[72]Negro World 14:25 (4 August 1923), p. 2.

[73]Negro World 13:3 (25 August 1922), p. 12.

Garvey held a high regard for the importance of the Black church and pointed to the centrality of religion and of Black religious institutions in the work of the Universal Negro Improvement Association. In a speech setting the stage for the canonization of Jesus as the Black Man of Sorrows, he declared:

> Let it be understood, once and for all, that no constructive program for the Negro can be effective which underestimates the hold his religious institutions have upon him. The material without the spiritual is as bad as, nay, worse than the spiritual without the material. We must have the anchor of religion, but we must make certain that it is what we consider conscientious for us as Negroes. That is what is meant by that object in our constitution, which reads, . . . "to promote a conscientious spiritual worship among the native tribes of Africa", implying, of course, that we shall first promote it among ourselves. That is what is meant when in our Declaration of Rights we demand "freedom of religious worship". This means freedom in our theology, freedom in our ritual and freedom in the control of our ecclesiastical organizations. We demand the exercise of a conscientious, spiritual freedom for the reason that spiritual freedom is the basis of all other freedoms. "Ye shall know the truth and the truth shall make you free". And in the exercise of this freedom we claim the right to set forth theology as we under-stand.[74]

---

[74]Negro World 16:26 (9 August 1924)

Garvey's concept of the Black church came as a direct result of his encounter with the vision of Black men controlling their own institutions. It was Garvey's theology rather than his ecclesiology that undergirded the Universal Negro Improvement Association. In fact, there are strong indications that Garvey was actively opposed to the establishment of the African Orthodox Church, at least in so far as it was conceived as being integrally related to the Universal Negro Improvement Association.

Several contemporary Black theologians viewed the Black church in a manner different from that of Garvey. They saw the Black church as the center and focal point around which the Black race gathered for its identity and recognition. They were more concerned with the significance that the Black church had for Blacks historically, and the attempt to demonstrate its continued significance in today's Black community. For example, Benjamin Mays, Black educator and theologian, saw the Black church as a source of identity for Blacks. He contended that Black people had the opportunity to be recognized as somebody of value and dignity in the Black church. He further stated that it was the responsibility of the Black church to develop programs within the Black community to address the critical areas facing Black people.

E. Eric Lincoln portrayed the Black church as a symbol of freedom and an instrument to effect change in the society. He insisted that there was no disjunction between the Black church and the Black community, and saw the Black church as a "universal church" claiming and representing Blacks out of a long tradition that looked back to the time when there was only the Black church to bear witness to "who" or "what" a man was as he stood at the bar of his community. He affirmed the Black church as the sole nexus of real power, gathered or ungathered in the Black community.

Joseph Washington, Jr. portrayed the Black church as an amusement center for the disengaged, an arena for power politics, and an organ for recognition, leadership and worship. He presented the Black church as an instrument for the fulfillment of participation in every area of life.

James Cone spoke of the Christian church in

Black theology, and issued a threefold task of the
church. First, he called upon the church to proclaim
the reality of divine liberation, which he defined
as preaching the gospel by confronting the world
with the reality of Christian freedom. Second, he
challenged the church to activelt share in the
liberation struggle by making the gospel a social,
economic, and political reality. Third, he argued
that the church should serve as a visible manifestation that the gospel is a reality, that is,
the church must live according to its preaching. It
was Cone's view that the participation in divine
liberation placed the church squarely in the context
of the world, a world where White and Black live,
encountering each other, the latter striving for a
little more room to breathe, and the former doing
everything possible to destroy Black reality. Cone
was disenchanted with both the Black and White
churches that failed to become involved in the
societal liberation of Black people.

Deotis Roberts portrayed the Black church as
a religious and community organization. He contended
that Blacks needed a cohesive institution to over-
come family disorganization and the social
c oncomitants of the same, and therefore saw the
Black church as fulfilling that primary need. He
pointed out that the Black church has the possibilities for restoring unity and peoplehood to the
Black community. His understanding of the Christian
faith led him to speak of both liberation and
reconciliation as proper goals for the Christian
church in general and of the Black church in
particular. Therefore, he declared that the Black
church, in setting Black people free, may make
freedom possible for white people as well. He
challenged the Black church to be an agent of
reconciliation, but also to be a visible fellowship,
an institution, an organization with economic, social,
and political influence. He regarded the Black
church as an extension of the Black family, and the
Black family as an extension of the Black church.

Most of the contemporary Black theologians
treat the subject matter of the Blackchurch from the
prespective of the historical role of the Black church
as an institution for religious, political, social,
and economic liberation in the Black community.
Cone and Roberts proposed a theology for the Black
church, with social, political and economic

implications. Mays, Washington and Eric Lincoln
emphasized the historical significance of the
Black church, and argued for its continuation as
an instrument to address and fulfill all areas of
Black life.

Albert Cleage was an exception. He called for
a theological as well as structural overhauling of
the traditional Black church. He created an
institution which he named the Shrine of the Black
Madonna, and presented a programmatic outline for
the Black church, both doctrinal and structural.
He referred to the new directions for the Black
church as Black Christian Nationalism. He called
for the restructuring of the Black church in terms
of its historical analysis, its Biblical interpretation, its theology, its ritual, and its
preaching:

> Instead of telling Black people
> about escaping from the world
> and going home to God on high,
> the Black church must begin to
> involve Black people in the
> Black Liberation Struggle by
> using the teachings of Jesus
> in the Synoptic Gospels, and
> the Old Testament concept of
> nation, to show Black people
> how coming together with Black
> pride and Black power is basis
> to survival. The Black church
> must become central in the
> Black Revolution. Jesus was a
> Black Messiah not in terms of his
> death on Calvary, but in terms of
> his dedication to the struggle of
> Black people here on earth.

> When we take the sacrament of Holy
> Communion it symbolizes our total
> rededication to personal partici-
> pation in the struggle of Black
> people and total rededication to the
> Black Nation. The Sacraments and
> ritual of the church then become for
> Black people an intrinsic part of the

revolutionary struggle.[75]

Cleage contended that a revolutionary Black church must be a place to which people come with pride, knowing that Jesus was Black, that the Nation Israel was Black, and that Black people are following in the footsteps of a Black Messiah. He called for the restructuring of the Black church that it may become the foundation on which Black people can build the Black Christian Nationalist Liberation Struggle and the emerging Black Nation. He restructured theology in order to make it something that Black people can understand and appreciate.

Although Cleage adopted the rituals and symbols used by Garvey, he differed from Garvey, in the sense that he operated within the confines of the institutional Black church which he created. Garvey called for a Black ecumenism which he referred to as a Christian confraternity. This concept was embodied in the Universal Negro Improvement Association. Garvey did not advocate the creation of a Black church, or the renewal of the Black church. Furthermore, he did not stress the significance of the role, or the importance of the Black church in the Black community. Instead, he called for the collective gathering of the Black race in the United States, England, the West Indies, Canada, France and Africa, into a Christian Confraternity, for the expressed purpose of redeeming the Black race:

> We shall march out, yes, as Black
> American citizens, as Black British
> subjects, as Black French citizens,
> as Black Italians, or as Black
> Spaniards, but we shall march out
> with a greater loyalty, the
> loyalty of race. We shall march out
> in answer to the cry of our fathers,
> who cry out to us for the redemption
> of our own country, our motherland
> Africa. We shall march out with
> a history of peace before and be-
> hind us, surely that history shall
> be our breastplate, for how can man

---

[75]Cleage, Black Christian Nationalism, pp. 41-42.

fight better than knowing that
the cause for which he fights is
righteous? Shall we not fight
for the glorious opportunity of
protecting and forever more
establishing ourselves as a
mighty race and nation, never
more to be disrespected by men.
Glorious shall be the battle when
the time comes to fight for our
people and our race. We should say
to the millions who are in Africa
to hold the fort, for we are
coming 400,000,000 strong.[76]

Garvey sought to cast the Universal Negro
Improvement Association into an all-embracing role
which included the institutionalization of a Black
civil religion, as opposed to the creation of an
institutional Black church. The movement possessed
its own meeting halls, its own order of worship as
set forth in the Negro Ritual, its distinctive set
of beliefs as outlined in the Negro Catechism, and
even special holidays of its own creation. The
beliefs and rituals of the Universal Negro
Improvement Association, however, were of a sufficiently high level of generality so that in
assenting to them one continues to adhere to
particular doctrines and practices of the separate
Black denominations; and one could still attend
those churches on Sunday mornings while participating
in the Universal Negro Improvement Association
activities on Sunday evenings. Garvey focused on
theology rather than ecclesiology. The sumbols,
rituals, and beliefs constituted a Black civil
religion rather than contributed to the institution
of a Black church. Garvey's primary goal was the
upliftment of the Black race and the redemption of
Africa. Therefore, the beliefs, rituals, and symbols
of the Universal Negro Improvement Association
served as a vehicle for national solidarity among
the Black race.

Finally, adapting Paschal, we can say of Black
theology as published by the contemporary Black

---

[76]Garvey, Philosophy of Opinions, I, p. 100.

theologians on the American scene, that it is not worth as much as Garvey's one act of faith, hope, charity and love, leading to an active effort to liberate the Black race. Contemporary Black theology seems to be hedged around with definitions, and built up into a symmetry of a system--but for Garvey theology was a living, operative, and renovating power in society. It was fire in the individual heart and a fireplace in the midst of the Black community. Garvey's theology is visceral rather than intellectual, irrational rather than rational; it is art rather than logic; spirit rather than form; primitive rather than contemporary.

The theology of Garvey is a commitment to the thrust that certain chapters of theology can only be written afterwards. It is a development of norms that should govern the Black race's conduct in the world. Garvey encountered the Black race in the riches of their personality, hence a theology that is both theocentric and anthropocentric.

Chapter VI

CONCLUSION: GARVEY'S CONTRIBUTION TO
BLACK AMERICA

In the African understanding of history, man
looks back from whence he came, and man is certain
that nothing shall bring this world to a conclusion.
There is no concept of history moving forwards
to a future climax, or to a better future, or to an
end of the world. The future does not dominate
African thinking. African history is really a
history of origins or genesis, and it forms the
foundation for the nation's existence. The African
theologian J.S. Mbiti captured the African concept
of time when he wrote:

> The Future has no independent
> existence of its own, since the
> events that compose Time have not
> occurred in it, and once they occur
> it is no longer Future but the
> Present and the Past. To Africans,
> Time has to be experienced to make
> sense. Therefore the essence of
> Time is what is Present and what
> is Past. Time moves backwards
> rather than forwards, from the
> Now (Present) to the Past. These
> two dimensions are the dominant
> Periods in the life of the
> individual, the community, the
> nation and humanity at large.[1]

Garvey approached Black Americans as children of
captivity looking forward to a new, yet ever old
land of their African forefathers, the land of God's
crowning glory. It was this concept of origin that
was rooted in Garvey's vision of Black Zionism, and
which was very much characteristic of African
thought. It was Garvey's understanding of African
history that undergirded his challenge to Black
Americans--"Up, You Mighty Race".

---

[1]J.S. Mbiti, "African Concept of Time," _African
Theological Journal_ (Mukumira, Tanzania), No. 1,
February 1968; pp. 8-20.

Religion to the Africans was far more than
ritual reflecting beliefs, but a reality reflected
in their actual way of life. Religion from the
earliest times became the dynamic force in the
development of all the major aspects of Black
civilization. According to African tradition, the
origin of man exhibits one common factor: man was
created by God and that he has his origin in Him.
This concept of God as Creator dominates African
religious thought, and provides for a pragmatic
theological estimate of man in African belief system.
Man, having been created in the image of God, draws
his very life-essence from God; but he also main-
tains a vital relationship with nature, the deities,
ancestors, the tribe, the clan, the entended family,
and himself.

Father Tempels, Anthropologist and Historian,
suggested the term "vital force" in order to explain
that dynamic element within the context of the total
life of the African community. He explained his
phenomenon of the universal vital force in stating
that:

> Man is one of these resultant living
> forces, created, maintained and
> developed by the vital, creative
> influence of God. At his own
> level, man, by the divine force,
> is himself a living force. Man
> is not the first or creative cause
> of life, but he sustains and adds
> to the life of the forces which he
> finds below him within his
> ontological hierarchy. And therefore,
> in Bantu thought, man, although in a
> more circumscribed sense than God, is
> also a casual force of life.[2]

Janheinz Jahn, African cultural Anthropologist
and Historian found the term "vital force"
fascinating for explaining or systematizing certain
aspects of African beliefs. He contended that
human individuals come into this--being as a result
of cosmic "life-force" or "vital force", acting upon

---

[2]Fr. Placide Tempels, Bantu Philosophy (Paris,
Presence, 1959), p. 65.

the biological union of "shadow" and "body" as
united with the spiritual life; "for the production
of a human being is a process of body and spirit.
The principle which assists in every beginning of a
human creature . . . Biological life . . . he shares
with the animal, but spiritual life divides from
the animal."[3]

Religion for Garvey was a phenomenon universally
experienced, and he insisted that no man ought to
criticize another either for holding to religion in
general or for believing in a particular conception
of the deity. Garvey drew from the African belief
system, and constantly urged his followers to worship
God through the spectacles of Ethiopia. Speaking
at the Sixth International Convention of the
Universal Negro Improvement Association, Garvey
declared:

> Man is a religious being, that is to
> say, he must have some kind of
> belief . . . call it superstition
> or what not. Man who has started
> to think traces his origin beyond
> man; and as such has been groping
> in the dark to find out the source
> from whence he came, and by our
> own intuition we have attributed that
> source to something beyond us; and
> in so believing we accept the idea
> of a religion. Some make our God
> the God of Fire; some make our
> God the God of Water; some make
> our God the God of the Elements and
> others of us accept the Christian
> belief. Man's religion is something
> we cannot eliminate from his system
> or destroy in him; therefore, it is
> folly for any man to go about
> attacking another man's religion,
> because to him it is fundamental.
> You may be a Christian; you may be
> a Mohammedan; that is your religion.
> We are all entitled to our own
> religious belief. Some of us are
> Catholics, some of us are
> Presbyterians, some of us are
> Baptists, and we deem it a right

158

to adhere to our particular belief.[4]

While Garvey was thus content to have his followers remain within any religious organization, whether Protestant or Catholic, Christian or non-Christian, he was not willing for them to retain the religious ideals or conceptualizations of another race. He, therefore, developed categories, and sought self-consciously to interpret the Christian faith which was his heritage, in the light of African symbols, rituals, and belief system. It was this historical and cultural/religious perspective of the African tradition and belief system which Garvey contributed to Black America and which made him the pre-eminent Black theologian and champion of the liberation of Black Americans.

Garvey arrived in the United States of America at a time when migration to the north was in full swing. He saw this occasion as an opportunity for Black Americans to rebuild, to resettle in the African tradition of nomads moving after destruction of villages to a new territory. James Weldon Johnson, the American Black Poet captured this movement most appropriately in the Black National Anthem, "Lift Every Voice and Sing":

> We have come over a way that
> With tears have been watered.
> We have come treading the path
> Of the blood of the slaughtered.
> Out of the gloomy past, till we
> have come at last,
> True to our God, true to our
> native land.[5]

It was in the midst of this migratory movement that Garvey arrived on the scene with his challenge to Blacks to negate the idea that they were inferior, and made repeated efforts at gaining their freedom,

---

[4]"Speech of Marcus Garvey Outlining Discussion on Formulating of Plans to Unify the Religious Beliefs and Practices of the Entire Negro Race", The Blackman (Kingston), August 1929, p. 13.

[5]James Weldon Johnson, The Books of American Negro Spirituals, (New York, 1925), I, p. 13.

and took definite and unceasing action to help give their history its distinctive shape.

What Garvey presented was not The Plan, but A Plan, a new beginning from a new vantage point in the history of the Black Race. Garvey responded to the Harlem Renaissance period with a posture toward a higher spiritual life and harked back to the primitive church and to African history, thus avoiding an activism or immediatism of which so many accused him. He challenged Black Americans to seize the reins of their destiny and shake free from the present servitude as a symbol of the inherent power which resided in them as creatures created in God's image.

What may have failed is the Plan, not the vision; for Garvey's contribution as a Black reformer was an attempt to reverse the trend of viewing Blacks as victims of history and as inferior, and he applied his whole being to that task. He found himself in an irreversible position, much like Martin Luther and the Protestant Reformation. Hence Garvey can now be regarded as one of the Black pioneers to the movement of Black Power and Black self-identity that swept America in the 1960's and 1970's. In this same manner Garvey can also be regarded as the pre-eminent Black theologian of the twentieth century.

Garvey's special contribution in the field of theology can provide the contemporary Black theological students with a different point of departure in their approach to Black theology. His basically theocentric approach is a critical reflection on the Black race's presence and activity in the world, in the light of God-given attributes and the reflection on the Black race's role in human/divine history, as creatures created in God's image--"the mighty race". His theology, unlike the theology of most contemporary Black theologians, did not lead to Garvey's commitment and action on behalf of the Black race, but is rather a reflection of that total commitment of his life to the struggle of a redeemed Africa. It was an eschatological vision that became operative, a creative hope that confronted the social realities of his day, and a fermenting enthusiasm that aroused millions of Black Americans to rally behind Garvey. Garvey had such an impact on the lives of his followers that

the Chaplain General of the African Orthodox Church
wrote of Garvey:

> No man has spoken to us like this
> man, inculcating pride and nobility
> of race, and clearly pointing out
> the Star of Hope to a discouraged
> and downtrodden people.[6]

Garvey's most significant contribution to the
Black church in America can be referred to as his
pastoral approach to the needs, hopes, and
aspirations of the Black race. In the seeming
absence of any pronounced ecclesiology in the
contemporary Black theological dissertations, with
the exception of Cleage's Shrine of the Black Madonna,
Garvey's call for a Christian confraternity included
the development of a pastoral theology.

Garvey's aim was the development and nurture of
a Christian community of a specific culture, at a
particular period in human history, confronted by
its own proglems and aspirations. In the formulation
of Garvey's theology for that community he
emphasized work, individual self-reliance, and a
rejection of fatalism. He reminded his followers
of the Divine injunction which stated that the
time would come when every man and every race must
return to its own "vine and fig tree". It was
Garvey's contention that the Black race, as creatures
created in the image of God and therefore members of
the great human family, must exercise their own
initiative and influence in their own protection.
Garvey insisted that they must contribute to the
uplift and up-building of their own race, so that
they may be able to enter into the new era as
partakers of the joys to be inherited, and added:

> Lagging behind in the van of
> civilization will not prove our
> higher abilities. Being sub-
> servient to the will and caprice of
> progressive races will not prove
> anything superior in us. Being

---

[6]A Speech by Bishop George McGuire in The Negro
Churchman, (September, 1923), p. 1.

satisfied to drink of the
dregs from the cup of human progress will not demonstrate our
fitness as a people to exist
alongside of others, but when
of our own initiative we strike
out to build industries, governments,
and ultimately empires, then and only
then will we as a race prove to our
Creator and to man in general that
we are fit to survive and capable
of shaping our own destiny.[7]

Garvey admonished his followers to secure
power of every kind in order to be respected among
other races. It was Garvey's view that a race
without authority and power was a race without
respect. He declared:

Power is the only argument that
satisfies man. Except the
individual, the race or the
nation has POWER that is
exclusive, it means that that
individual, race or nation will
be bound by the will of the other
who possesses this great
qualification . . . Hence it is
advisable for the Negro to get
power of every kind. POWER in
education, science, industry,
politics and higher government.
That kind of power that will
stand out signally, so that other
races and nations can see, and if
they will not see, then FEEL.[8]

Garvey warned the Black race not to use power to
oppress the human race but to use their strength
physically, morally, and otherwise to preserve
humanity and civilization.

---

[7]Garvey, _Philosophy of Opinions_, I, pp. 8-9.

[8]_Ibid._, p. 22.

At a time in the United States of America when
the concept of Black Power is still a source of
group pride and expectations, Garvey's contribution
to the Black American struggle must be seen in
historical perspective. It was a seed that was
planted, and has now borne some fruit in the form
of disciples or students of Garvey. Among such
disciples includes Noble Drew Ali, Elijah Muhammed,
Malcolm X, and Dr. Martin Luther King Jr., men who
were inspired by his dynamic leadership. Referring
to the Black Muslim Movement and the ex-Moorish
Science Moslems movement, C. Eric Lincoln said:

> The older people who do belong
> to these movements, especially
> in the Northern cities, are for
> the most part ex-Garveyites . . .
> Many of these older "nationalists"
> consider Noble Drew Ali and
> Muhammad as natural successors
> to Garvey, and they have had little
> difficulty in making the transition.
> Muhammad himself professes "a
> very high opinion" of both Garvey
> and Noble Drew Ali; he refers to
> them as "fine Muslims" and calls
> upon their sympathizers to follow
> him and cooperate in the work
> because they were only trying to
> finish up what those before them
> started.[9]

The followers of Marcus Garvey are represented in
the Muslim temples in substantial numbers, as are
the Moorish scientists.

Less than eight months before his assassination
in New York on February 21, 1964, Malcolm X, in an
interview with Yael Lotan, Jamaican Journalist, said
of his parents' involvement in the Garvey movement
and their pride in their African heritage:

> You will find that most West Indians,
> most people in the Caribbean area,
> are still proud that they are black,

---

[9]C. Eric Lincoln The Black Muslims in America
(Beacon Press, Boston, 1961), p. 23.

proud of the African blood, and
their heritage; and I think this
type of pride was instilled in
my mother, and she instilled it in
us, too, to the best degree she
could. She had--despite the fact
that her father was white--more
African learnings, and African
pride, and a desire to be
identified with Africa. In fact
she was an active member of the
Marcus Garvey movement. My
father, besides being an active
worker in the Marcus Garvey movement,
was a Christian clergyman--a
Baptist minister.[10]

Regarding Marcus Garvey's influence on his life,
Malcolm X in the same interview volunteered this
opinion:

Every time you see another nation
on the African continent become
independent, you know that Marcus
Garvey is alive. It was Marcus
Garvey's philosophy of Pan
Africanism that initiated the
entire freedom movement, which
brought about the independence of
Africa nations. And had it not
been for Marcus Garvey, and the
foundations laid by him, you
would find no independent nations
in the Caribbean today . . .

All the freedom movements that
are taking place right here in
America today were initiated by
the work and teachings of Marcus
Garvey. The entire Black Muslim
philosophy here in America is
feeding upon the seeds that were

---

[10]Yael Lotan, "Daily Gleaner", (Jamaica, W. I.,
July 12, 1964), p. 3.

planted by Marcus Garvey.[11]

Dr. King Jr. was inspired by Garvey's sense of commitment and his ability to mobilize the masses of Black people. King recognized the work Garvey had started and pledged to continue his efforts in the struggle for Black liberation. In a speech at a reception at the National Stadium in Jamaica Dr. King praised Garvey for his contribution to the Blacks in America. King laid a wreath at Marcus Garvey's shrine in Jamaica in June 1965, and said, in part:

> Marcus Garvey was the first man of color in the history of the United States to lead and develop a mass movement. He was the first man, on a mass scale, and level, to give millions of Negroes a sense of dignity and destiny, and make the Negro feel that he was somebody.
>
> You gave Marcus Garvey to the United States of America, and he gave to the millions of Negroes in the United States a sense of personhood, a sense of manhood, and a sense of somebodiness. As we stand here let us pledge ourselves to continue the struggle in this same spirit of somebodiness . . . in the conviction that all God's children are significant . . . that God's black children are just as significant as His white children. And we will not stop until we have freedom in all its dimensions.[12]

Like Dr. King, Garvey too had a dream. It was a dream that was rooted in the eventual liberation of the Black race. In Garvey's own words:

---

[11] Ibid., p. 4.

[12] Ibid., p. 4.

No one knows when the hour
of Africa's Redemption cometh.
It is in the wind. It is
coming. One day, like a storm,
it will be here. When that
day comes all Africa will stand
together.[13]

In another passage Garvey said:

All of us may not live to see
the higher accomplishment of
an African Empire--so strong
and powerful, as to compel
the respect of mankind, but
we in our lifetime can so
work and act as to make the
DREAM a possibility within
another generation.[14]

Garvey's dream which seemed impossible in his
life-time is now the stimulation for a new Black
nationalism. It still sweeps the lanes of Black
life everywhere. It is obscured by fictitious
names--Black Power, Black is Beautiful, Black
Capitalism and Black Culture. But credit needs to
be given to Garvey for his vision, as he often said
that the Black race is determined if it takes
eternity, to win the cause of freedom. Garvey came
to America endowed with an extraordinary ability
for organization and leadership, and an undaunted
faith in the possibilities of the Black race. To
this end, he committed his life and instilled a
spirit of hope in the Black race that cannot be
extinguished as long as they live and have their
beings among others.

In the American context Garvey was more the
symbol of a peculiar mood in Black Americans than
the inspirer of it. In that sense he has succeeded
in articulating some of the long crushed and unformed
desires of the Black masses, thereby contributing to

---

[13]Garvey, Philosophy of Opinions, I, p. 10.

[14]Ibid., p. 14.

their self-awareness and self-identity. The themes
he developed were not new, rather, they were drawn
from a long tradition of Black theological reflection
upon the experience of Black Americans. It was for
this very reason that Black clergymen from a wide
range of denominational backgrounds were attracted
to the Universal Negro Improvement Association.

Several of the denominational leaders openly
supported and endorsed Garvey's leadership and even
encouraged their clergy and members to join the
Garvey movement. For instance, of the one hundred
twenty-two men and women who on August 20, 1920
signed the "Declaration of Rights" which was the
charter document of the Universal Negro Improvement
Association and African Communities League, fully
one-sixth of them were clergy.

Junius C. Austin, the minister who was
selected to speak at the opening session of the
Third International Convention (1922) "Representing
the Negro Ministry", was one of several nationally
prominent Baptist clergymen who were Garvey
enthusiasts. He was regarded by his peers as
"America's greatest Pulpit Orator". It was doubtless
for this reason that Garvey invited him to address
the convention. Austin rose to the occasion with a
stirring defense of the Universal Negro Improvement
Association, and culminated his speech with a
ringing endorsement of Marcus Garvey:

> We have a just cause and we have
> faith in the justice of God. Most
> of all we have among our assets a
> Moses (Marcus Garvey) whom we can
> trust. He is not a spy; he comes
> not as a traitor nor a hired
> servant for foes, but is
> appointed by God and is recognized
> and accepted among the leaders of
> the race and is going to lead us on
> to victory![15]

---

[15]Negro World 12:26 (8 August 1922), p. 7.

Austin's church, Pilgrim Baptist Church in Chicago, which reportedly had a membership of upwards of five thousand, served as a forum for the discussion and advancement of Garvey's program.

A second nationally know Baptist clergyman who surpassed even Austin in terms of his militancy and outspoken criticism of white racism, and who also for a period of time was an active Garveyite, was the Reverend William H. Moses. He was Pastor of the Zion Baptist Church in Philadelphia, and was also corresponding secretary of the National Baptist Church of the USA. Moses led the parade of prominent New York City clergymen who spoke out in Garvey's behalf. He was invited to speak on the platform at Liberty Hall and full speech was printed in the Garvey's newspaper, the New World, 21 July, 1923. In an exegesis of two Old Testament passages, Chronicles 12:32 and Joel 2:28, 29 which he applied directly to Marcus Garvey, Moses said:

> And who is the one who understands
> his time? He is the man upon whom
> God has poured out his spirit. The
> young man who according to Joel will
> see visions, while the old men dream
> dreams. If the spirit of God is not
> on Marcus Garvey, it is not on any-
> body else. Mr. Garvey can truly say:
> "The Spirit of the Lord is upon me.
> He hath anointed me to open the eyes
> of the blind and preach the acceptable
> word of the Lord." Today is this
> scripture fulfilled. Right here
> today I want to say this, that God's
> spirit is poured out in a simple
> way on the world.[16]

He insisted that prophets do not come from ranks of the educated or the priestly class, and informed his hearers that Garvey had more to say than all the Black preachers in the world. Moses further declared:

> You may talk about you come from
> Harvard and "I come from Yale"

---

[16]*Negro World* 14:23 (21 July 1923), p. 2.

and "I come from Cornell" but
the man that speaks to the
multitude must come from Heaven.
He is not born in a day. No man
can make him. He comes out of
the groaning and travail of ages.
Mr. Garvey is the pent-up feeling
of the race that has been in the
region of the shadow of death for
ages.[17]

His speech concluded with an eloquent description of
the vision which he had glimpsed from the podium in
Liberty Hall:

I see a time when Black people
everywhere are going to rise and
shine, for the lie is given and
the Light of God is shining on
the books. I see a larger day.
I see a city ofschools and
churches. I see cities everywhere, extending from the Cape
of Good Hope to Cairo in Egypt.
I see a crowd yonder extending
from the Zambesi to the Niger
River. I see this race of mine
walking up, hand in hand, American
and what not, pressing on together,
have a home together. Let nobody
deceive you. It may take a year.
It may take ten thousand years.
But under God the hour will come
when Ethiopia shall stretch forth
her hand unto God and Black men
shall hold their heads high, and
the name of Marcus Garvey shall
be embalmed in our memories and our
children's memories.[18]

In 1924 Bishop Reverdy C. Ransom of the African
Methodist Episcopal Church, one of the most able,

_____

[17]Ibid., p. 10.

[18]Ibid., p. 11.

articulate, and outspoken of the AME leaders in the first half of the twentieth century, commented publicly on the career and program of Marcus Garvey. He referred to Garvey as a prophet and martyr, and declared:

> He proclaims for the unity and solidarity of the Black people throughout the world. He pleads that we put into commission and organization the intellectual financial, professional and industrial resources of the entire race and use this power to participate in the redemption and development of the continent of Africa . . .
>
> As a prophet, Mr. Garvey has run true to form by meeting the age-long rewards of the prophet . . . he has been stoned, he has been imprisoned and now he has been banished. But truth, aspirations and ideals can neither be imprisoned nor deported.[19]

Ransom was also Editor-in-Chief for the AME Church Review, and his numerous sympathetic editorials defending the program of Garvey over the years increased respect for the Universal Negro Improvement Association among the many clergymen of the AME Church.

Lelia Walters, the wife of an African Methodist Episcopal Zion Bishop, an officeholder of the Universal Negro Improvement Association, was a strong advocate for Garvey. She was also an ardent supporter of the right of women to express themselves and to play a role in the Universal Negro Improvement Association. On one occasion, at a banquet held in honor of Marcus Garvey on the eve of one of his tours through the United States, she rose to speak concerning the guest of honor:

---

[19]"Marcus Garvey Mightiest Prophet", Pittsburgh Courier (17 December, 1927), p. 4., reprinted in Negro World 23:20 (24 December, 1927), p. 2.

Ladies and gentlemen,it is a
pleasure for me to be here tonight.
Last night I was at a great meeting
where they discussed the cause of
Gandhi and the great nationalist
movement in India under his
leadership. As I sat there and
listened to this cause expounded and
set forth my mind was drawing
comparisons between the Gandhi
movement and our own great
movement, the Universal Negro
Improvement Association, under the
leadership of Marcus Garvey. There
they spoke very feelingly of the
outstanding leaders of mankind
coming down the line from Hannibal,
Napoleon, George Washington,
Toussaint L'Ouverture, and as no
one spoke of our own great leader,
Hon, Marcus Garvey, I thought that
a serious omission had been made.
To my mind he has reached the
pinnacle of fame and is the most
outstanding figure in the world
of mankind today. To him I say,
"Carry on Marcus Garvey. Thy
great work that will lead others to
their goal and thy name shall be
sacred in the annals of history."[20]

Mrs. Walters was not an uncritical supporter of the
Universal Negro Improvement Association as
evidenced on one occasion when she took the
organization to task for not allowing sufficient
expression for women within the movement.

In the third major branch of Black Methodism,
the Colored (Christian) Methodist Episcopal Church,
Dr. William Yancey Bell, pastor of the prestigious
Williams Institutional CME Church in New York City,
stood out as an articulate defender of Marcus
Garvey. Bell contended that brotherhood could be
achieved among the races, but saw a prerequisite

_____

[20]Negro World 12:8 (8 April, 1922), p. 2.

171

goal, namely, brotherhood within the race. In a speech which he delivered in Liberty Hall in August 1923, while Garvey was incarcerated in the Tombs Prison, Bell expressed the principle of brotherhood:

> There is also a hope. And I speak
> here tonight neither as pro or
> anti anything. I speak first of
> all as a Negro interested in
> Negroes. This is the hope--that
> in the fullness of time a Negro
> has arisen with faith enough to
> believe and courage enough to
> attempt to prove that Negroes
> universally could be taught to
> forget their differences.
> Inspired to hope and nerved to
> strive for a better and
> brighter day when the world would
> be compelled to admit again that
> Negroes can function successfully
> elsewhere than at the woodpile
> and well. It may not require an
> inspired seer, a Pittsburgh
> lawyer, nor a Wall Street broker
> to find a flaw in the plan or
> system of the UNIA but when it
> comes to the matter of Ethiopia's
> awakening and of Ethiopia's
> organization, you've simply got to
> hand it to Marcus Garvey.[21]

Bell was elected Bishop of the CME Church in 1938 and served actively in that post for twenty-four years. He insisted that genuine Christianity was essentially brotherhood, and characterized the Universal Negro Improvement Association as a move-ment committed to race redemption.

Arnold Josiah Ford, founder of one of the first Black Jewish groups in the United States, was a very early Garvey supporter. He was present as a signer

---

[21]William Y. Bell, "The Christian Spirit in Race Redemption", delivered in Liberty Hall, August 1923. Negro World 14:26 (11 August, 1923), p. 8.

of the 1920 Declaration of Rights, and he also held
the post of Choirmaster and Bandmaster of the
Universal Negro Improvement Association. Ford
brought into the Garvey movement a very large
membership from his congregation. Theodore Vincent,
in his book <u>Black Power and the Garvey Movement</u>,
said of Ford:

> A sizable minority of New York
> Garveyites were Black Jews--
> some six hundred marched in a
> special contingent of the 1922
> convention parade, and Rabbi J.
> Arnold Ford, the Association's
> musical director, had adopted
> Judaism long before he joined
> the Garvey movement, bringing
> most of his Beth B'nai Congregation
> with him.[22]

Garvey also had supporters among the clergy and
members of the Ethiopian Coptic Church. Such
supporters included Rev. S.B. Barbour, Philadelphia;
Bishop Edwin H. Collins, New York; and Rev. Joseph
Josiah Cranston of Baltimore. The latter had been
a signatory of the 1920 Declaration of Rights.[23]

However, there was that side of Garveythat led
him to undertake gigantic concerns. In some cases
he appeared egotistical and wedded to great ideals.
Garvey was more of a visionary and a man of
philosophies, theologies, and opinions, rather than
a practical man of affairs. Indeed, his visions of
the future of the race, influenced by some extent
by the romantic humanitarian picture of a
regenerated Africa, were so splendidly grand as to
bear no relation as to what was probable. He never
seemed to have thought out the practical implications
of his ideas, although he was unswervingly committed
to them. He gave little thought to the problems

----

[22]Theodore Vincent, <u>Black Power and the Garvey
Movement</u> (New York, 1971), pp. 134-135.

[23]<u>Negro World</u> 9:12 (6 November, 1920), p. 10.

of the organization of the mass exodus for which he
so devoutly wished, the settle of immigrants, and
of the conflicts physical and cultural, that any
massive emigration to an already peopled land
would bring.

Garvey was not without his critics. A New York
World reporter, who had studied Garvey while reporting his conventions and trial, described him in a
Sunday issue of the newspaper, June 1923, as a
group psychologist and idealist planner, but not
practical. On the one hand, he praised Garvey's
unusual ability to mobilize the masses:

> Marcus Garvey can lay claim to
> being a most successful student
> of group psychology. His powers
> to weld Negroes,--heterogeneous
> in thought and environment--into
> one solid phalanx, working for
> the same ideals, have been almost
> uncanny. A forceful and convincing
> speaker, nimble-minded in debate,
> and seldom permitting himself to
> be put on the defensive; it is an
> interesting study watching him
> exercise complete mastery over
> a gathering of from three to
> five thousand of his followers.[24]

On the other hand, in the same article the reporter
pointed to another side of Garvey's character:

> Conceiving and attempting to put
> over big things is his specialty.
> Even Harlem with more than
> 180,000 Negroes has only come
> within the range of his mental
> calculations merely as a spoke
> in the wheel. Few of his ideas
> ever reached the stage of fruition,
> but this was not because all of
> them were devoid of merit. There
> were some deserving of favourable

---

[24]New York World (7 June, 1923), p. 3.

consideration. But idealism
is one thing, the application of
practical methods is another.
With him practicability very
often had to give way to idealism
and egotism.[25]

Leonard E. Barrett, Professor of Religion at Temple
University in Philadelphia, reflecting on Garvey's
ability as a mass leader, contended that Garvey
was not an ordinary man: he was a man of dreams,
fantastic dreams, gigantic and spectacular dreams;
a rare man indeed. Barrett, however, saw a dilemma
between Garvey's role as a visionary and that of an
organizer, and declared:

> One of the main downfalls of the
> movement (UNIA), was Garvey's
> effort to fulfill both roles, that
> of the visionary and the practical
> organizer. This was a mistake.
> Garvey was a dreamer, an idealist,
> a prophet, a man of charisma; the
> routinization of the movement needed
> more levelheaded men to carry out
> those dreams. The prophet or the
> messianic leader, by nature, is
> scarcely prepared for day-to-day
> routine.[26]

In an article to the Jamaica Standard, January
26, 1939, Randolph Williams, formerly employed by
the Universal Negro Improvement Association, was
also harshly critical of Garvey:

> Like Frankenstein, he discovered
> late that he had created a hugh thing,
> that he alone could not manage, and
> that he could not trust others to
> help him with, fearing that his
> helpers, not understanding the

------

[25]Ibid., p. 3.

[26]Leonard E. Barrett, Soul-Force, (Garden City,
New York, 1974), p. 144.

intricate mechanism of this thing
would destrou it. He had worked
out a programme that needed a few
generations for its completion,
something that was no one-man's
job; he attempted to accomplish
it in a single generation, and
chiefly by himself. He suffered
from great impatience, and was
constantly mortified that others
could not give themselves up as
completely to the Cause as he
could. Because of this great
impatience, when he should have
put all the resources of his
huge Association behind one single
project, and put it over, he
tackled half a dozen and succeeded
with none.[27]

Garvey was featured in several news articles across
the world as he became the world storm center of
his race's fight for equality.

The attitude of the Black intellectuals of
Garvey's day was rather harsh towards him.
Especially his foremost critic Dr. W.E.B. Du Bois,
who, in Crisis, November 24, 1924, wrote:

The American Negroes have endured
this threat all too long with fine
restraint and every effort to
cooperation and understanding.
But the end has come. Every
man who apologizes for or defends
Marcus Garvey (who was in prison)
from this day forth writes himself
down as unworthy of the countenance
of decent Americans. As for Garvey
himself, this open ally of the KKK
should be locked up or sent home.[28]

---

[27]Jamaica Standard, (Kingston, Jamaica,
January 26, 1939), p. 3.

[28]Crisis, (November 24, 1924), p. 5.

These were harsh words coming from a Black leader,
but the sentiments portrayed the depth of hatred
and disdain that was engendered among the
intellectuals by the Garvey movement. Dr. George
W. Bagnall, another intellectual of Garvey's day
characterized Garvey in this manner:

> A Jamaican of unmixed stock, squat,
> stocky, fat and sleek, with pro-
> truding jaws, and heavy jowls, small
> bright pig-like eyes and rather
> bulldog-like face. Boastful,
> egotistic, tyrannical, intolerant,
> cunning, shifty, smooth and suave,
> avaricious . . . gifted at self-
> advertizement, without shame in
> self-landation . . . without
> regard for veracity, a lover of
> promp and tawdry finery and
> garish display.[29]

Yet, for all the castigations of his many
critics, several of them honored Garvey years after
his death, and affirmed his contribution to Black
America, as well as other peoples across the world.
W.E.B. Du Bois, who, ironically, found refuge in
the Africa Garvey had fought so hard for, finally
acknowledged that Garvey was an extraordinary leader
of the masses. In his last days in Africa, Du Bois
reflected on the Garvey movement:

> It was a grandiose and bombastic
> scheme, utterly impracticable as
> a whole, but was sincere and had
> some practical features; and
> Garvey proved not only an
> astonishingly popular leader but
> a master propagandist. News of
> his movement and of his promise
> and his plans, reached Europe and

---

[29]Dr. George W. Bagnall in a discourse entitled,
"The Madness of Marcus Garvey", quoted in Edmund
Cronon, Black Moses (Madison, Wisconsin, 1948),
p. 107.

Asia, and penetrated every corner
of Africa.[30]

In his book Black Manhattan, James Weldon Johnson of
"Harlem Renaissance" fame both praised and damned
Garvey:

> He had the energy and daring and
> Napoleonic personality--the
> personality that drew masses of
> followers. He stirred the
> imagination of the Negro masses
> as no Negro ever had. He
> raised more money in a few years
> than any other Negro organization
> had and ever dreamed of. He had
> great power and great possibilities
> within his grasp. But his
> deficiencies as a leader
> out-weighed his abilities.[31]

In later years some of Garvey's original critics
and opponents became defenders of his movement. E.
Franklin Frazier, in 1926, commenting upon Garvey
and his movement wrote:

> As a leader of a mass movement
> among Negroes, Garvey has no
> equal.[32]

Later, in 1949, Frazier described Garvey as being:

> The leader of the most important,
> though emphemeral, nationalistic
> movement among Negroes.[33]

---

[30]W.E.B. Du Bois, Dusk of Dawn (New York, 1940),
pp. 277-278.

[31]James Weldon Johnson, Black Manhattan (New
York, 1930), p. 285.

[32]Nathan Huggins, Voices From the Harlem
Renaissance, (New York, 1976), p. 32.

[33]John Henrik Clarke, ed., Marcus Garvey And The
Vision of Africa, (New York, 1974), p. 198.

The Black historian A. Philip Randolph, at one time
one of Garvey's most severe critics, in later years
analyzed Garveyism in this manner:

> A word about the value of
> Garveyism to Negroes today. It
> has done some splendid things.
> It has inculcated into the
> minds of Negroes and need and
> value of organization. It has
> also demonstrated the ability of
> Negroes to come together in
> large masses under Negro leader-
> ship. Of course, the A.M.E.
> Church has done as much; so have
> the Negro Secret Orders.
> Garveyism, also, has conducted
> wholesome, vital, necessary
> and effective criticism on
> Negro leadership. It has stimulated
> the pride of Negroes in Negro
> history and traditions, thereby
> helping to break down the slave
> psychology which throttles and
> strangles Negro initiative, self-
> assertiveness, ambition, courage,
> independence, etc. It has further
> stiffened the Negro's backbone to
> resist the encroachments and insults
> of white people. Again, it has
> emphasized the international
> character of the Negro problem.
> As a propaganda organization, at
> one period of its history, it was
> highly useful in awakening Negro
> consciousness to the demands of the
> times.[34]

Garvey's contribution to Black America was also
noted and affirmed by his fellow Jamaicans. In
addition, his impact on an international level was
recognized by leaders of nations across the world.
For example on November 5, 1956, at a rally in
Jamaica where the bust of Marcus Garvey was placed
in the main park, the Honorable Norman Manley, Chief

---

[34]Nathan Huggins, Voices From the Harlem
Renaissance, p. 32.

Minister of the Jamaican House of Representatives,
gave an address in which he said:

> I am particularly glad that Mr.
> Marcus Garvey's widow--Mrs. Amy
> Jacques Garvey, is with us on
> this platform. I am sure that
> if her husband were alive, he
> would have noted with pride the
> great strides that the Negro
> peoples of the world have made
> in the last twenty-five years,
> and moreso in the fields where he
> laboured. Since Garvey dreamed
> his great dream in American
> considerable progress has been
> made by the people whom he
> sought to serve, and at this
> moment they are witnessing in
> the USA what is verily believed
> to be the end, the last stage of
> the struggle of millions of Negro
> people there, to achieve complete
> equality in that land.[35]

At that same rally, William Sherrill, President-
General of the Universal Negro Improvement
Association said of Garvey:

> When viewing the individual and
> his work, one whose greatness and
> achievements extend far beyond
> the boundaries of this Island,
> we ask ourselves--was the world
> different because he lived? The
> answer to this question as it
> relates to Marcus Garvey places
> him in the company of the Great.
> Because Garvey lived, Jamaica is
> different; because Garvey lived,
> Negro America is different;
> because Garvey lived, Africa is
> different. His work and teaching
> gave birth to a New Negro, A New
> Africa, and this impact went a long

---

[35]The Daily Gleaner, (Jamaica, November 5, 1956),
p. 1.

way in shaping a New World. For
his cry was not alone. "Africa
for the Africans", but Asia for
the Asiatics" and "Palestine for
the Jews". He did more to cry-
stallize National sentiment in
so-called backward countries than
any single individual of our time.
Measured by the standard of
change Garvey and his teachings
have wrought in the world, Garvey
rises to the heights of greatness.[36]

Marcus Garvey was never privileged to set foot on
African soil, but he had a great yearning for that
great continent. He had a deep consciousness of
the need to awaken in the hearts of the Black race
a sense of belonging to a people striving to impress
their image and personality on a world, in terms of
freedom, justice and peace for all. In commemorating
Garvey's birthday, a Jamaican journalist, Frank Hill,
writing in the Daily Gleaner, under the heading
"The Prophet of Black Zionism" wrote in part:

What makes a man great? It is, I
think, the universal quality of
the contribution he makes to the
civilization of his times. The
accent is on the word universal,
for the quality of his vision
must be of such as to be able to
hold the attention of mankind, rather
than mere isolated pockets of men
grouped in special circumstances.
Garvey's message lighted new hope
as much among the wandering
Negroes, as among the wandering
Negroes, as among the cringing
tribesmen of the Africa plains . . .

What was ths significance of Garvey?
The Prophet of Black Zionism beat
the drums for the ingathering to
Africa. He may have meant it as

---

[36]Amy Jacques Garvey, Garvey and Garveyism
(New York, 1970), p. 297.

> a summons for a physical recall.
> But the message went more deeply,
> more enduringly than that. Eyes
> and hearts and minds turned to
> Africa--to the new values and
> standards and principles that
> earned their validity from the
> culture that grew out of the
> African community.[37]

Peter Abrahams, a South African author, in a political analysis of the colonial situation in the 1950's, reflected on Garvey's contribution:

> Marcus Garvey gave to the Negroes
> of the twentieth century a sense
> of self-awareness, a sense of pride
> and dignity that largely overcame
> the inferiority complex bred by
> centuries of racial and colour
> oppression.
>
> And since the first state in any
> kind of liberation is the liberation
> of the mind, Marcus Garvey can
> justly be regarded as a primary
> source of the great freedom
> movements in the colonial world
> today. And that Jamaica honors
> him shows the extend to which
> Jamaica has changed.[38]

Chief Nana Kobina Nketsia, Director of the Institute of Art and Culture in Ghana visited Jamaica, July 1965. In placing a wreath at the shrine of Marcus Garvey, he unloosed his sandals, and with bare feet, he bowed before the tomb, and performed absolution with water and devotion according to his spiritual ritual. Then he said:

----

[37]Frank Hile, _Daily Gleaner_ (Kingston, August 17, 1960), p. 2.

I am pleased to be present at this
sacred spot where Marcus Garvey my
international leader isenshrined.
Seeing you, my brothers and sisters,
gathered here in your hundreds to
pay homage, inspires me to higher
endeavor as a noble descendant
of a proud African race.   I
sincerely believe our mission for
freedom is not an accident of
history, but the work of Divine
Providence, being manifested
through the ages.   Through UNITY
among Africans, the Black man's
place in the world is secured for
all times, despite misfortunes
brought by opposition forces.
Thanks be to God and Marcus
Garvey's teachings for the light
that is shining over Africa today,
and will always shine.[39]

Garvey's contribution to Black America and to the
world cannot be underestimated. His commitment to
promoting the advancement of his race was complete,
and he unflaggingly continued his efforts as best
as he knew, inspite of and despite the opposition
levelled against him. No wonder that even his
critics during his time, had words of commendation
for Garvey in latter years.

Mr. Dennis Ejindu, an African journalist
reviewing the book, "Garvey and Garveyism", wrote:

Garvey's aim was to destroy the
conventional inferiority complex
of the Negro and prove that the
Negro is more than capable of
designing his own future and
fortune.

He was furiated by the exploitation
everywhere of the Black man, and
therefore decided that the Black man
should grab a chance to improve his

---

[39]Garvey, Garvey and Garveyism, pp. 315-316.

lot, and ultimately to fashion
a civilization worthy of human
dignity. For this Garvey was
feared and hated by the
governments of Europe and America,
who hounded and destroyed him.
But not before Garveyism had
intoxicated more than two
million followers all over the
world, who henceforth re-echoed
his theme of African for the
Africans.[40]

Several African leaders were greatly influenced by
Marcus Garvey, and acknowledged his contribution to
the African peoples. Dr. Kwame Nkrumah, former
Prime Minister of Ghana, speaking at the closing
session of the All-African People's Conference in
Accra, stated in part:

It was warned us that so many of
our brothers from across the seas
are with us. We take their presence
here as a manifestation of the keen
interest in our struggle for a free
Africa. We must never forget that
they are a part of us.

These sons and daughters of Africa
were taken away from our shores, and
despite all the centuries which have
separated us, they have not forgotten
their ancestral links.

Many of them made no small contribution
to the cause of African freedom. A
name that springs immediately to mind
in this connection is Marcus Garvey.
Long before many of us were even
conscious of our own degradation,
Marcus Garvey fought for African

---

[40]Dennis Ejindu, "Garvey and Garveyism", Morning
Post, (Ghana, 18 February 1966), p. 4.

national and racial equality.[41]

George Padmore writing in the Jamaica Gleaner on the former Prime Minister of Kenya, Jomo Kenyatta described the impression that Garvey made on Kenyatta in this manner:

> Kenyatta met Marcus Garvey and became converted to the philosophy-- "Africa for Africans", and after Garvey's death Kenyatta and other Africans and West Indians formed the Pan African Federation, and called a Congress at Manchester, England in 1945 to plan a broad strategy of African liberation.
>
> Kenyatta returned to Kenya in 1946 to assume leadership of the African Union. Within one year over 100,000 members were enrolled. In the following year Nkrumah returned to the Gold Coast to lead West African nationalism. Other Pan-African leaders returned to South and Central Africa to organize political parties, trade unions and co-operatives.[42]

Rev. Clarence Harding, Commissioner to Africa for the Universal Negro Improvement Association, reporting on the impact that Marcus Garvey had on Joseph Mobutu, a former President of the Republic of Congo said:

> I arrived in the capital city of Kinshasa. I was met by the Deputy Minister of Foreign Affairs--Mr. Bokondo. I was taken to the Patrice Lumumba Hotel. The following morning I was escorted

---

[41](A Speech before the All-African People's Conference in Accra), Morning Post, (Ghana, 13 December 1958), p. 2.

[42]George Padmore, "The Man with the Burning Spear", Jamaica Gleaner, (Kingston 23 October, 1952), p. 3.

> to the Presidential Palace,
> where I was received by President
> Mobutu. He is a staunch admirer
> of Marcus Garvey, and was surprised
> to know that the U.N.I.A. was still
> in operation (in 1967). I spoke
> to him about our problems, and the
> opposition by groups and
> governments. He said that he fully
> understood our position, and that
> our survival was a miracle, but a
> blessing to Africa.[43]

In a conversation with President Jomo Kenyatta, Mrs.
Amy Garvey, wife of Marcus Garvey, reported that
she was informed by Kenyatta that when he was a
young man he met Garvey in London, heard him speak
several times, and considered himself a member of
the Universal Negro Improvement Association.

Another African leader, Dr. Kaunda, President
of Zambia, reported how he was deeply influenced by
Garvey. Kaunda shared that insight with a delegation
from the branch of the Universal Negro Improvement
Association in Jamaica, who welcomed him to Jamaica
in November 1966. In a report from the delegation
which was published in the Jamaica Star it stated
in part:

> A delegation from the Universal
> Negro Improvement Association
> consisting of Messrs. E.E. Whyte,
> Vin Bennett, J.P., Rev. K.A. Bailey,
> met President Kenneth Kaunda at
> King's House yesterday morning,
> and presented him with an address
> on behalf of the Association.
>
> Dr. Kaunda thanked the delegation,
> and said how much the teaching of
> Marcus Garvey, the founder of the
> U.N.I.A. had helped him to build
> his NEW NATION. He expressed the
> hope that the U.N.I.A. would

---

[43]Garvey, Garvey and Garveyism, pp. 319-320.

continue in the work to inspire
Africans at home to obtain their
freedom.[44]

Kaunda's slogan which he used for his native country
Zambia was in keeping with Garvey's motto for the
Universal Negro Improvement Association:

> One Africa! One Nation! To the
> Africans Garvey was more than a
> Black mass leader in America, he
> was a symbol of the eventual
> redemption and autonomy of
> African nations. Garvey made all
> peoples of African descent
> political aspirants for the
> continent of Africa and the
> West Indies, and he made his
> impact while making his
> contribution to Black America.

Whatever may be said of Garvey, in terms of his
contribution to Black America, these two factors
are clear--he demonstrated that Blacks can be mobi-
lized, and that Blacks are eager to repose confidence
in, and support committed, Black leadership. Garvey
had the unusual ability and personality that drew
masses of followers. He revived the power of the
human spirit in Black people everywhere. His
significance lay in the fact that he embodied and
directed a new spirit of independence among Black
Americans. Whatever may have happened to his
grandios schemes of finance and politics, Garvey had
the unusual capacity to inspire others.

In conclusion, as the pre-eminent Black theologian
of the twentieth century, Garvey undoubtedly did
much to vindicate his race and dispel the myth of
inherent Black inferiority. Consequently, as the
most articulate and brilliant vindicator of the
Black race in the twentieth century, Garvey's ideas
have contributed greatly to the historical roots of
the contemporary Black power and Black theological
movements. He was by no means a systematic

---

[44]Jamaica Star, (Kingston, 23 November, 1966),
p. 1.

theologian, in the sense of carefully setting forth
a unified or definitive statement concerning his
doctrine of God, of Christ, of man, and of man's
destiny. However, the attempt of this dissertation
was to demonstrate that there was a unity to
Garvey's thought, and that he self-consciously sought
to interpret the Christian faith which was his
heritage in the light both of his people's experience,
and in order to hasten the building up of the morale
of the Black race.

SELECTED BIBLIOGRAPHY

A. Primary Sources:

1. Books

Garvey, Amy Jacques. Garvey and Garveyism. Collier-McMillan Ltd., London, 1963.

Garvey, Marcus. Philosophy and Opinions of Marcus Garvey. Edited by Amy Jacques Garvey. Vol. I., Universal Publishing House, New York, 1923.

_____. Philosophy and Opinions of Marcus Garvey or Africa for the Africans. Edited by Amy Jacques Garvey. Vol. II., Universal Publishing House, New York. 1926.

_____. Selections from the Poetic Meditations of Marcus Garvey. Edited by Amy Jacques Garvey. Universal Publishing House, New York, 1927.

_____. The Tragedy of White Injustice. Edited by Amy Jacques Garvey. Universal Publishing House, New York, 1927.

2. Documents

Constitution and Book of Laws Made for the Government of the Universal Negro Improvement Association, Inc., and African Communities League Inc., of the World. Universal Press, New York, 1918, revised and amended August, 1922.

Ford, Arnold Josiah. The Universal Ethiopian Hymnal. Beth B'nai Abraham Publishing Co., New York, 1921.

Garvey, Marcus. Aims and Objects of The Movement for The Solution of The Negro Problem Outlined. Press of the Universal Negro Improvement Association, New York, 1921.

_____. "The Negro's Greatest Enemy", Current History Magazine. xviii (September, 1963), 951-57. (Autobiographical Material)

McGuire, George Alexander, compiled. The Universal Negro Catechism. Press of the Universal Negro Improvement Association, New York, 1921.

_____, compiled, The Universal Negro Ritual. Press of the Universal Negro Improvement Association, New York, 1921.

Speeches, Articles, Pamphlets and Notes of Marcus Garvey from Newspaper and Magazine clippings located in:

Calendar of the Manuscripts in the Schomburg Collection of Negro Literature, compiled by the Historical Records Survey Work Projects Administration, Andronicus Publishing Company, Inc., New York, 1942.

Dictionary Catalog of the Schomburg Collection of Negro Literature and History, The New York Public Library, Vol. IV. G-T., G.K. Hall and Company, Boston, Massachusetts, 1962.

B. Secondary Sources:

Books and Articles dealing with Garvey and the Garvey Movement

Barrett, Leonard E. Soul-Force. Anchor Press/ Doubleday, New York, 1974.

Becker, William. "Black Power in Christian Perspective". Religion and Life, Vol. XXXVIII, (1969).

_____. "A Black Moses and His Dream of a Promised Land", Current Opinion, LXX (March, 1921).

Brawley, Benjamin G. The Negro Genius: A New Appraisal of the Achievement of the American Negro in Literature and the Fine Arts. N.Y., Dodd, Mead, 1937.

Brisbane, Robert Hughes, Jr. "Some New Light on the Garvey Movement" Journal of Negro History, XXXVI (January, 1951).

Burkett, Randall K. Black Redemption: Churchmen
    Speak For The Garvey Movement. Temple
    University Press, Philadelphia, 1978.

Clarke, John Henrik, ed. Marcus Garvey and the
    Vision of Africa, Vintage Books, New York, 1974.

Cronon, Edmund Davis. Marcus Garvey. Prentice Hall,
    Inc. Englewood Cliffs, N.J. 1973.

_____. Black Moses, The Story of the
    Universal Negro Improvement Association.
    University of Wisconsin Press, Madison, 1955,
    1962.

Davis, Daniels, Marcus Garvey. Franklin Watts, Inc.,
    New York, 1972.

Du Bois, W.E.B. "Marcus Garvey", Crisis, XXI, 58-60
    (December, 1920), and (January 1921).

_____. "The U.N.I.A.", Crisis, XXV. (January,
    1923).

Elmes, A.F. "Garvey and Garveyism: An Estimate",
    Opportunity, III. (May, 1925).

Frazier, E. Franklin. "Garvey: A Mass Leader"
    Nation, CXXIII. (August 18, 1926).

Harris, Robert. Black Glory in the Life and Times
    of Marcus Garvey. African Nationalist Pioneer
    Movement, New York, 1961.

Johnson, Charles S. "After Garvey: What?"
    Opportunity, I (August, 1923).

Maglandgbayan, Shawna. Garvey, Lumumba, Malcolm.
    Third World Press, Chicago, 1972.

McKay, Claude. "Garvey as a Negro Moses", Liberator,
    IV (April 1922).

Miller, Kelly. After Marcus Garvey: What of the
    Negro?" Contemporary Review, CXXXI (April 1927).

Nembhard, Len S. Trials and Triumphs of Marcus Garvey. Kingston, Jamaica: Gleaner, 1940.

Pickens, William. "Africa for the Africans: The Garvey Movement", Nation, CXIII (December 28, 1921).

_____. "The Emperor of Africa: The Psychology of Garveyism", Forum, LXX (August, 1923).

_____. "Marcus Garvey", New Republic, LII (August 31, 1927).

Rose, Arnold M. The Negro's Morale: Group Identification and Protest. Minneapolis: Univ. of Minnesota.

Rushing, Byron. "A Note on the Origin of the African Orthodox Church" Journal of Negro History, Vol. 57, (January, 1972).

Streator, George. "Three Men: Napier, Moton, Garvey, Negro Leaders who Typified an Era for their People", Commonweal, XXXII (August 9, 1940).

Truttle, Worth M. "Garveyism: Impressions from a Missionary School", World Tomorrow, IV. (June, 1921).

Vincent, Theodore G. Black Power and The Garvey Movement. Ramparts Press, New York, 1971.

Walrond, Eric D. "Imperator Africans-Marcus Garvey: Menace or Promise?" Independent; CXIV (January 3, 1925).

White, Gavin. "Patriarch McGuire (ChaplainOGeneral of Marcus Garvey's U.N.I.A.) and the Episcopal Church" Historical Magazine of Protestant Episcopal Church, Vol. XXXVIII, (1969).

2. Black Theology and Current Black Theologians

Balthazar, Eulalio. The Dark Center: A Process Theology of Blackness. Panlist Press, New York, 1973.

Cleage, Albert. The Black Messiah. Sheed and Ward, New York, 1968.

_____. Black Christian Nationalism. Morrow, New York, 1972.

Cone, James H. Black Theology and Black Power. The Seabury Press, New York, 1969.

_____. A Black Theology of Liberation. J.B. Lippincott Company, New York, 1970.

_____. God of The Oppressed. The Seabury Press, N.Y., 1975.

Dobin, Arthur, "A History of The Negro Jews in America", unpublished paper, City College of the City University of New York, Schomburg Collection, New York City Public Library, 1965.

Drake, St. Clair. The Redemption of Africa and Black Religion. Third World Press, Chicago, 1970.

Fauset, Arthur. Black Gods of The Metropolis. University of Pennsylvania Press, Philadelphia, 1944.

Evarts, Arrah B. "Color Symbolism". Psychoanalytic Review. Vol., 6, 1919.

Gardiner, J. and J. De Otis Roberts Sr., (eds.,), Quest For A Black Theology. United Church Press, Philadelphia, 1971.

Gergen, Kenneth, "The Significance of Skin Color in Human Relations", Color and Race. ed., J.H. Franklin, Beacon Press, Boston, 1968.

Frazier, E. Franklin. The Negro Church in America. Schocken Books, New York, 1963.

Jones, William. "Theodicy and Methodology in Black Theology: A Critique of Washington, Cone, and Cleage". Harvard Theological Review, Vol. 64, 1971.

King, Martin Luther. Where Do We Go From Here?
Harper and Row, Publishers, New York, 1967.

Landes, Ruth. "Negro Jews in Harlem", Jewish
Journal of Sociology, IX, December, 1967.

Lincoln, Eric. The Black Experience in Religion.
Anchor Books, Anchor Press/Doubleday, Garden
City, N.Y., 1974.

_____. The Black Muslims in America. Beacon
Press, Boston, 1973.

_____. The Black Church Since Frazier.
Schocken Books, New York, 1974.

Mays, Benjamin. The Negro's God. Atheneum, N.Y.,
1968.

Mays, Benjamin E. The Negro's Church. Negro
Universities Press, New York, 1969.

Mitchell, Henry H. Black Preaching. J.B. Lippincott
Company, Philadelphia and New York, 1970.

Nettleford, Rex M. Mirror, Mirror: Identity, Race
and Protest in Jamaica. William Collins and
Sangster Ltd., Jamaica, 1970.

Roberts, J. Deotis, Liberation and Reconciliation:
A Black Theology. Westminister Press,
Philadelphia, 1971.

_____. A Black Political Theology.
Westminister Press, Philadelphia, 1974.

Sterling, Dorothy. The Making of An Afro-American:
Martin Delany, 1812-1885. Doubleday, Garden
City, 1971.

Terry-Thompson, Arthur Cornelius. The History of
The African Orthodox Church. Beacon Press,
New York, 1956.

Thomas, Latta R. Biblical Faith and The Black
American. Judson Press, Valley Forge, 1976.

Thurman, Howard. The Luminous Darkness. Harper & Row Publishers, N.Y., 1965.

Turner, H.M. "God is A Negro", Black Nationalism in America, Bobbs-Merrill, N.Y., 1970.

Ullman, Victor. Martin R. Delany: The Beginnings of Black Nationalism. Beacon Press, Boston, 1971.

Washington, Joseph R. Black Sects and Cults. Doubleday and Co., Inc., 1972.

_____. The Politics of God. Beacon Press, Boston, 1967.

Wilmore, Gayraud. Black Religion and Black Radicalism. Doubleday, Garden City, N.Y., 1972.

Woodson, Carter G. The History of the Negro Church. The Associated Publishers, Washington, 1921.

3. Primitivism: African Roots

Blyden, Edward. African Life and Customs, Humanities, New York, 1967.

_____. Christianity, Islam, and The Negro Race. HumAnities, New York, 1967.

Campbell, Joseph. The Masks of God: Primitive Mythology. The Viking Press, New York, 1957.

Degraft-Johnson, J.C. African Glory. Walker, New York, 1956.

Janheinz, Jahn, Mantu. Faber, London, 1961.

Jochannan, Josef ben. Africa: Mother of Western Civilization. Alkebu-Lan, New York, 1970.

_____. African Origins of the Major Western Religions. Alkebu-Lan, New York, 1970.

_____. Black Man of The Nile. Alkebu-Lan, New York, 1970.

Lynch, Hollis. Edward Wilmot Blyden: Pan-Negro
    Patriot. Humanities, New York, 1967.

Manoedi, M. Kokete. Garvey and Africa. New York
    Age, New York, 1970.

Mbiti, John S. African Religions and Philosophy.
    Praegers Publishers, Inc., New York, 1969.

_____. Concepts of God in Africa. Praegers
    Publishers, Inc., New York, 1970.

_____. "African Concept of Time", African
    Theological Journal (Mukumira, Tanzania), No. I.,
    February, 1968.

Padmore, George. Pan-Africanism or Communism.
    Doubleday and Company, New York, 1971.

Rogers, J.A. Africa's Gift to America. Rogers, New
    York, 1961.

Evans-Pritchard, E.E. Theories of Primitive Religion,
    Oxford, 1965.

Shepperson, George, "Ethiopianism and African
    Nationalism". Phylon, Vol. XIV., 1953.

Smith, E.W., ed. African Ideas of God. London, 1950.

Thompson, Vincent B. Africa and Unity: The
    Evolution of Pan-Africanism. Humanities, New
    York, 1969.

C. Bibliography of Bibliographies

Amos, Preston E. One Hundred Years of Freedom: A Selected Bibliography of Books about the American Negro. Washington Association for the Study of Negro Life and History, 1963.

Ellis, Ethel M. Vaughan. The American Negro: A Selected Checklist of Books. Including a List of Periodicals, Films and Film Strips, Recordings, and Agencies that distribute Free and Inexpensive Materials. Washington, D.C., Negro Collection Howard University, 1968.

Krash, Ronald, Juris Gail, Dennis Duke assisted by the Reference Staff of Pius XII Library. Black America: A Research Bibliography. St. Louis University, Pius XII Library, St. Louis, Missouri, 1972.

Porter, Dorothy B. A Working Bibliography on the Negro in United States. University Microfilms, A Xerox Company, Ann Arbor, Michigan, 1968.

Schatz, Walter. Directory of Afro-American Resources, R.R. Bowker Company, New York and London, 1970.

Smith, Dwight L. Afro-American History: A Bibliography. American Bibliographical Center-Calio Press, Inc. Santa Barbara, California, 1944.